Psychology on the Net

Allyn and Bacon

Psychology on the Net
2001 Edition

Fred W. Whitford
Montana State University

Doug Gotthoffer
California State University–Northridge

Allyn and Bacon
Boston • London • Toronto • Sydney • Tokyo • Singapore

Executive Editor: Carolyn Merrill
Multimedia Editor: Nina Tisch
Editorial Production: Marla Feuerstein
Cover Creative Director: Kate Conway
Cover Designer: Amy Braddock
Editorial Production Service: Omegatype Typography, Inc.

NOTICE: Between the time Web site information is gathered and then published, it is not unusual for some sites to have ceased operating. Also, the transcription of URLs can result in unintended typographical errors. The Publisher would appreciate notification where these occcur so that they may be corrected in subsequent editions. Thank you.

In its effort to provide a diverse list of Web sites, the Publisher has included links that do not necessarily represent the views of Allyn and Bacon. Faculty, students, and researchers are strongly advised to use their analytical skills to determine the truth, accuracy, and value of the content in individual Web sites.

TRADEMARK CREDITS: Where information was available, trademarks and registered trademarks are indicated below. When detailed information was not available, the publisher has indicated trademark status with an initial capital where those names appear in the text.

Macintosh is a registered trademark of Apple Computer, Inc.

Microsoft is a registered trademark of Microsoft Corporation. Windows, Windows95, and Microsoft Internet Explorer are trademarks of Microsoft Corporation.

Netscape and the Netscape Navigator logo are registered trademarks of Netscape Communications Corporation.

ISBN 0-205-32965-9

Printed in the United States of America

10   9   8   7   6   5   4   3   2   1   03   02   01   00

Contents

Part 1   Introduction to the Internet

Part 2   Psychology Activities

Psychology on the Net

Introduction to the Internet

You're about to embark on an exciting experience as you become one of the millions of citizens of the Internet. Once you've accustomed yourself to this wonderful new world, you'll be amazed by how much you can discover, learn, and accomplish as you explore the Internet's dynamic resources.

Some Things You Ought to Know

Much of the confusion over the Internet comes from two sources. One is terminology. Just as the career you're preparing for has its own special vocabulary, so does the Internet. You'd be hard pressed to join in the shoptalk of archeologists, librarians, or carpenters if you didn't speak their language. Don't expect to plop yourself down in the middle of the Internet without some buzzwords under your belt, either.

The second source of confusion is that there are often many ways to accomplish the same ends on the Internet. This is a direct by-product of the freedom so highly cherished by Net citizens. When someone has an idea for doing something, he or she puts it out there and lets the Internet community decide its merits. As a result, it's difficult to put down in writing the *one exact* way to send email or find information on slugs or whatever.

In addition, there are differences in the workings of a PC or Mac and the various versions of the two major browsers, Netscape Communicator (or Navigator) and Internet Explorer. If you can't find a particular command or function mentioned in the book on your computer, chances are it's there, but in a different place or with a slightly different name. Check the manual or online help that came with your computer, or ask a more computer-savvy friend or professor.

And relax. Getting up to speed on the Internet takes a little time, but the effort will be well rewarded. Approach learning your way around the Internet with the same enthusiasm and curiosity you approach learning your way around a new college campus. This isn't a competition. Nobody's keeping score. And the only winner will be you.

In *Understanding Media,* Marshall McLuhan presaged the existence of the Internet when he described electronic media as an extension of our central nervous system. On the other hand, today's students introduced to the Internet for the first time describe it as "Way cool."

No matter which description you favor, you are immersed in a period in our culture that is transforming the way we live by transforming the nature of the information we live by. As recently as 1980, intelligence was marked by "knowing things." If you were born in that year, by the time you were old enough to cross the street by yourself, that definition had changed radically. Today, in a revolution that makes McLuhan's vision tangible, events, facts, rumors, and gossip are distributed instantly to all parts of the global body. The effects are equivalent to a shot of electronic adrenaline. No longer the domain of the privileged few, information is shared by all the inhabitants of McLuhan's global village. Meanwhile, the concept of information as intelligence feels as archaic as a television remote control with a wire on it (ask your parents about that).

With hardly more effort than it takes to rub your eyes open in the morning you can connect with the latest news, with gossip about your favorite music group or TV star, with the best places to eat on spring break, with the weather back home, or with the trials and tribulations of that soap opera character whose life conflicts with your history class.

You can not only carry on a real-time conversation with your best friend at a college half a continent away, but you can see and hear her, too. Or, you can play interactive games with a dozen or more worldwide, world-class, challengers; and that's just for fun.

When it comes to your education, the Internet has shifted the focus from amassing information to putting that information to use. Newspaper and magazine archives are now almost instantly available, as are the contents of many reference books. Distant and seemingly unapproachable experts are found answering questions in discussion groups or in electronic newsletters.

The Internet also addresses the major problem facing all of us in our split-second, efficiency-rated culture: Where do we find the time? The

part

1

Internet allows professors and students to keep in touch, to collaborate and learn, without placing unreasonable demands on individual schedules. Professors are posting everything from course syllabi to homework solutions on the Internet, and are increasingly answering questions online, all in an effort to ease the pressure for face-to-face meetings by supplementing them with cyberspace offices. The Internet enables students and professors to expand office hours into a twenty-four-hour-a-day, seven-day-a-week operation. Many classes have individual sites at which enrolled students can gather electronically to swap theories, ideas, resources, gripes, and triumphs.

By freeing us from some of the more mundane operations of information gathering, and by sharpening our information-gathering skills in other areas, the Internet encourages us to be more creative and imaginative. Instead of devoting most of our time to gathering information and precious little to analyzing and synthesizing it, the Internet tips the balance in favor of the skills that separate us from silicon chips. Other Internet citizens can gain the same advantage, however, and as much as the Internet ties us together, it simultaneously emphasizes our individual skills—our ability to connect information in new, meaningful, and exciting ways. Rarely have we had the opportunity to make connections and observations on such a wide range of topics, to create more individual belief systems, and to chart a path through learning that makes information personally useful and meaningful.

part

1

A Brief History of the Internet

The 20th century's greatest advance in personal communication and freedom of expression began as a tool for national defense. In the mid-1960s, the Department of Defense was searching for an information analogy to the new Interstate Highway System, a way to move computations and computing resources around the country in the event the Cold War caught fire. The immediate predicament, however, had to do with the Defense Department's budget, and the millions of dollars spent on computer research at universities and think tanks. Much of these millions was spent on acquiring, building, or modifying large computer systems to meet the demands of the emerging fields of computer graphics, artificial intelligence, and multiprocessing (where one computer was shared among dozens of different tasks).

While the research was distributed across the country, the unwieldy, often temperamental, computers were not. This made it difficult for computer scientists at various institutions to share their computer work without duplicating each other's hardware. Wary of being accused of re-inventing the wheel, the Advanced Research Projects Agency (ARPA), the funding arm of the Defense Department, invested in the ARPANET, a private network that would allow disparate computer systems to communicate with each other. Researchers could remain ensconced among their colleagues at their home campuses while using computing resources at government research sites thousands of miles away.

A small cadre of ARPANET citizens soon began writing computer programs to perform little tasks across the Internet. Most of these programs, while ostensibly meeting immediate research needs, were written for the challenge of writing them. These programmers, for example, created the first email systems. They also created games like Space Wars and Adventure. Driven in large part by the novelty and practicality of email, businesses and institutions accepting government research funds begged and borrowed their way onto the ARPANET, and the number of connections swelled.

As the innocence of the 1960s gave way the business sense of the 1980s, the government eased out of the networking business, turning the ARPANET (now Internet) over to its users. While we capitalize the word "Internet", it may surprise you to learn there is no "Internet, Inc.," no business in charge of this uniquely postmodern creation. Administration of this world-wide communication complex is still handled by the cooperating institutions and regional networks that comprise the Internet. The word "Internet" denotes a specific interconnected network of networks, and not a corporate entity.

part

Using the World Wide Web for Research

Just as no one owns the worldwide communication complex that is the Internet, there is no formal organization among the collection of hundreds of thousands of computers that make up the part of the Net called the World Wide Web.

If you've never seriously used the Web, you are about to take your first steps on what can only be described as an incredible journey. Initially, though, you might find it convenient to think of the Web as a giant television network with millions of channels. It's safe to say that, among all these channels, there's something for you to watch. Only, how to find it? You could click through the channels one by one, of course, but by the time you found something of interest it would (1) be over or (2) leave you wondering if there wasn't something better on that you're missing.

A more efficient way to search for what you want would be to consult some sort of TV listing. While you could skim through pages more rapidly than channels, the task would still be daunting. A more creative approach would allow you to press a button on your remote control that would connect you to a channel of interest; what's more, that channel would contain the names (or numbers) of other channels with similar programs. Those channels in turn would contain information about other channels. Now you could zip through this million-channel universe, touching down only at programs of potential interest. This seems far more effective than the hunt-and-peck method of the traditional couch potato.

If you have a feel for how this might work for television, you have a feel for what it's like to journey around (or surf) the Web. Instead of channels on the Web, we have *Web sites*. Each site contains one or more *pages*. Each page may contain, among other things, links to other pages, either in the same site or in other sites, anywhere in the world. These other pages may elaborate on the information you're looking at or may direct you to related but not identical information, or even provide contrasting or contradictory points of view; and, of course, these pages could have links of their own.

Web sites are maintained by businesses, institutions, affinity groups, professional organizations, government departments, and ordinary people anxious to express opinions, share information, sell products, or provide services. Because these Web sites are stored electronically, updating them is more convenient and practical than updating printed media. That makes Web sites far more dynamic than other types of research material you may be used to, and it means a visit to a Web site can open up new opportunities that weren't available as recently as a few hours ago.

part

1

Hypertext and Links

The invention that unveils these revolutionary possibilities is called *hypertext*. Hypertext is a technology for combining text, graphics, sounds, video, and links on a single World Wide Web page. Click on a link and you're transported, like Alice falling down the rabbit hole, to a new page, a new address, a new environment for research and communication.

Links come in three flavors: text, picture, and hot spot. A text link may be a letter, a word, a phrase, a sentence, or any contiguous combination of text characters. You can identify text links at a glance because the characters are <u>underlined</u>, and are often displayed in a unique color, setting the link apart from the rest of the text on the page. Picture links

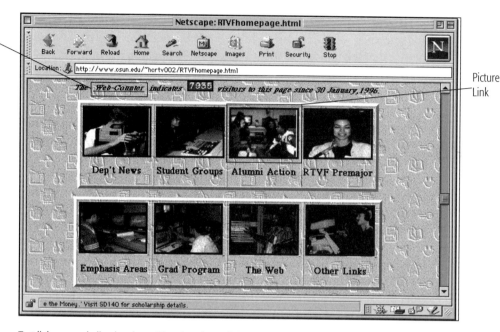

Text Link

Picture Link

Text links are underlined and set of in color. Picture links are set off by a colored border. Hot spots carry no visual identification.

are pictures or other graphic elements. On the Web, a picture may not only be worth a thousand words, but it may also be the start of a journey into a whole new corner of cyberspace.

The third kind of link, the hot spot, is neither underlined nor bordered, a combination which would make it impossible to spot, were it not for a Web convention that offers you a helping hand finding all types of links. This helping hand is, well, a hand. Whenever the mouse cursor passes over a link, the cursor changes from an arrow to a hand. Wherever you see the hand icon, you can click and retrieve another Web page. Sweep the cursor over an area of interest, see the hand, follow the link, and you're surfing the Web.

In the Name of the Page

Zipping around the Web in this way may seem exciting, even serendipitous, but it's also fraught with perils. How, for instance, do you revisit a page of particular interest? Or share a page with a classmate? Or cite a page as a reference for a professor? Web page designers assign names, or titles, to their pages; unfortunately, there's nothing to prevent two designers from assigning the same title to different pages.

An instrument that uniquely identifies Web pages does exist. It's called a Universal Resource Locator (URL), the cyber-signposts of the World Wide Web. URLs contain all the information necessary to locate:

- the page containing the information you're looking for;
- the computer that hosts (stores) that page of information;
- the form the information is stored in.

A typical URL looks like this:

```
http://www.abacon.com/index.html
```

You enter it into the **Location** or **Address** field at the top of your browser window. Hit the **Return** (or **Enter**) key and your browser will deliver to your screen the exact page specified. When you click on a link, you're actually using a shorthand alternative to typing the URL yourself because the browser does it for you. In fact, if you watch the "Location" or "Address" field when you click on a link, you'll see its contents change to the URL you're traveling to.

part

1

The URL Exposed

How does your browser—or the whole World Wide Web structure, for that matter—know where you're going? As arcane as the URL appears, there is a logical explanation to its apparent madness. (This is true not only of URLs but also of your computer experience in general. Because a computer's "intelligence" only extends to following simple instructions exactly, most of the commands, instructions, and procedures you'll encounter have simple underlying patterns. Once you familiarize yourself with these patterns, you'll find you're able to make major leaps in your understanding of new Internet features.)

To unscramble the mysteries of World Wide Web addresses, we'll start at the end of the URL and work our way toward the front.

```
/index.html
```

This is the name of a single file or document. Eventually, the contents of this file/document will be transferred over the Internet to your computer.

However, because there are undoubtedly thousands of files on the Internet with this name, we need to clarify our intentions a bit more.

```
www.abacon.com
```

This is the name of a particular Internet *Web server,* a computer whose job it is to forward Web pages to you on request. By Internet convention, this name is unique. The combination of

```
www.abacon.com/index.html
```

identifies a unique file/document on a unique Web server on the World Wide Web. No other file has this combined address, so there's no question about which file/document to transfer to you.

The characters *http://* at the beginning of the URL identify the method by which the file/document will be transferred. The letters stand for HyperText Transfer Protocol.

part

1

Quick Check

Don't Be Lost In (Hyper)Space

Let's pause for a quick check of your Web navigation skills. Look at the sample web page on the next page. How many links does it contain?

Did you find four? The four links include:

1. The word "links" in the second line below the seaside picture;

2. The sentence "What about me?";

3. The word "cyberspace" in the quick brown fox sentence;

4. The hot spot in the seaside picture. We know there's at least one link in the picture, because the cursor appears as a hand. (There may be more hot spots on the page, but we can't tell from this picture alone.)

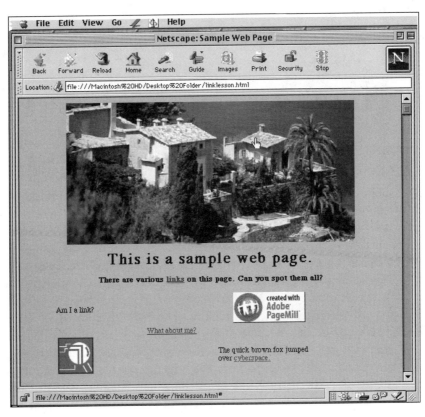

A sample web page to exercise your link identifying skills.

Getting There from Here

Now you know that a URL uniquely identifies a page and that links used as shorthand for URLs enable you to travel from page to page in the Web; but what if a link takes you someplace you don't want to go? Missing page messages take several forms, such as URL 404, Object not on this server, Missing Object, Page not Found, but they all lead to the same place—a dead end. The page specified by the link or URL no longer exists. There are many reasons for missing pages. You may have entered the URL incorrectly. Every character must be precise and no spaces are allowed. More than likely, though, especially if you arrived here via a link, the page you're after has been moved or removed. Remember, anybody can create a link to any page. In the spirit of the Internet, there are no forms to fill out, no procedures to follow. That's the good news. The bad news is that the owner of a page is under no

A missing page message, an all too common road hazard on the information superhighway.

obligation to inform the owners of links pointing to it that the page location has changed. In fact, there's no way for the page owner to even know about all the links to her page. Yes, the Internet's spirit of independence proves frustrating sometimes, but you'll find these small inconveniences are a cheap price to pay for the benefits you receive. Philosophy aside, though, we're still stuck on a page of no interest to us. The best strategy is to back up and try another approach.

Every time you click on the **Back** button, you return to the previous page you visited. That's because your browser keeps track of the pages you visit and the order in which you visit them. The **Back** icon, and its counterpart, the **Forward** icon, allow you to retrace the steps, forward and backward, of your cyberpath. Sometimes you may want to move two, three, or a dozen pages at once. Although you can click the **Back** or **Forward** icons multiple times, Web browsers offer an easier navigation shortcut. If you use Netscape, clicking on the **Go** menu in the menu bar displays a list of your most recently visited pages, in the order you've been there. Unlike the **Back** or **Forward** icons, you can select any page from the menu, and a single click takes you directly there. There's no need to laboriously move one page a time. If you use Internet Explorer, you can click on the **History** button in the Explorer bar to see a list of links you visited in previous days and weeks, or press the arrow at the end of the Address bar to see previously visited links.

part

1

Quick Check

As a quick review, here's what we know about navigating the Web so far:

- Enter a URL directly into the Location field;
- Click on a link;
- Use the **Back** or **Forward** icons;
- Select a page from the **Go** menu.

You Can Go Home (and to Other Pages) Again

How do we return to a page hours, days, or even months later? One way is to write down the URLs of every page we may want to revisit. There's got to be a better way, and there is: We call them bookmarks (on Netscape Communicator) or favorites (on Microsoft Internet Explorer).

Like their print book namesakes, Web bookmarks (and favorites) flag specific Web pages. Selecting an item from the **Bookmark/Favorites** menu, like selecting an item from the **Go** menu, is the equivalent of entering a URL into the **Location** field of your browser, except that items in the **Bookmark/Favorites** menu are ones you've added yourself and represent pages visited over many surfing experiences, not just the most recent one.

To select a page from your bookmark list, pull down the **Bookmark/ Favorites** menu and click on the desired entry. To save a favorite page location, use the Add feature available in both browsers. In Netscape Communicator, clicking on the **Add Bookmark** command makes a bookmark entry for the current page. **Add to Favorites** performs the same function in Microsoft Internet Explorer. Clicking this feature adds the location of the current page to your **Bookmark/Favorites** menu.

A cautionary note is in order here. Your bookmark or favorites list physically exists only on your personal computer, which means that if you connect to the Internet on a different computer, your list won't be available. If you routinely connect to the Internet from a computer lab, for example, get ready to carry the URLs for your favorite Web sites in your notebook or your head.

part

1

Searching and Search Engines

Returning to our cable television analogy, you may recall that we conveniently glossed over the question of how we selected a starting channel in the first place. With a million TV channels, or several million Web pages, we can't depend solely on luck guiding us to something interesting.

On the Web, we solve the problem with specialized computer programs called *search engines* that crawl through the Web, page by page, cataloging its contents. As different software designers developed search strategies, entrepreneurs established Web sites where any user could find pages containing particular words and phrases. Today, Web sites such as Yahoo!, AltaVista, Excite, WebCrawler, and HotBot offer you a "front door" to the Internet that begins with a search for content of interest.

The URLs for some popular search sites are:

Excite	`www.excite.com`
Yahoo!	`www.yahoo.com`
AltaVista	`www.altavista.digital.com`
WebCrawler	`www.webcrawler.com`
MetaCrawler	`www.metacrawler.com`
Infoseek	`www.infoseek.com`
HotBot	`www.hotbot.com`

Internet Gold Is Where You Find It

Let's perform a simple search using HotBot to find information about the history of the Internet.

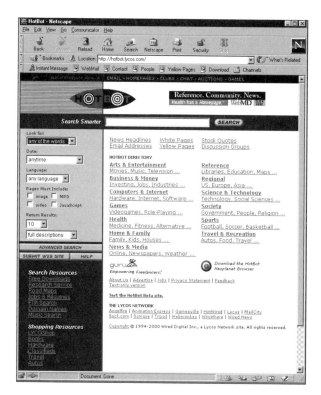

We'll start by searching for the words "internet" or "history." By looking for "any of the words," the search will return pages on which either "internet" or "history" or both appear.

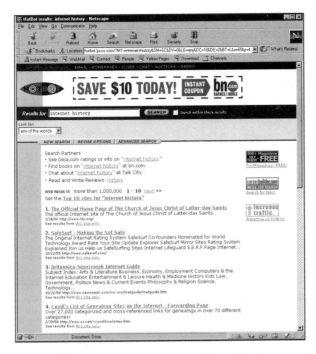

Our search returned more than 1,000,000 matches or *hits*. Pages are ranked according to the following factors: words in the title, keyword meta tags, word frequency in the document, and document length.

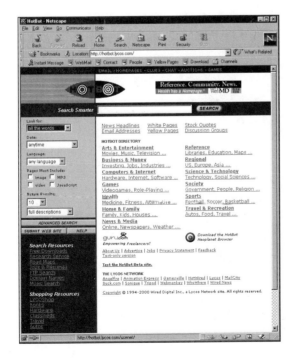

We can conduct the same search, but this time look for "all the words." The search will return hits when both "internet" and "history" appear on the same page, in any order, and not necessarily next to each other.

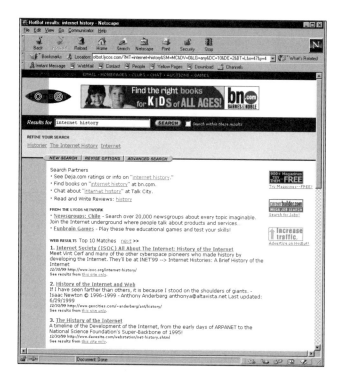

The search is narrowed down somewhat, but still has more than 1,000,000 hits.

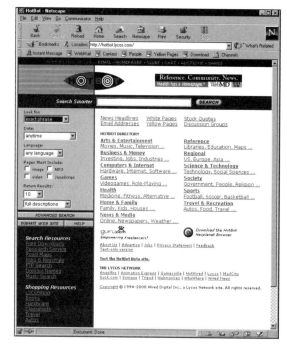

When we search for the exact phrase "internet history," which means those two words in exactly that order, with no intervening words, we're down to several thousand hits (still a substantial number).

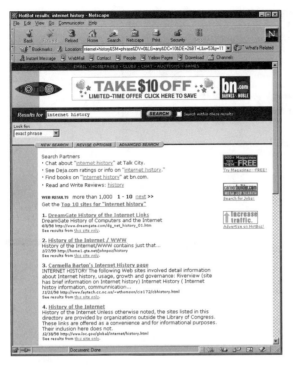

Now the first hits may be more specific. However, other hits in the list may have nothing to do with the history of the Internet. Hits happen. No search engine is 100 percent accurate 100 percent of the time. Spurious search results are the serendipity of the Internet. Look at them as an opportunity to explore something new.

Out of curiosity, let's try our history of the Internet search using a different search engine. When we search for the phrase "history of the internet" using WebCrawler, the quotation marks serve the same purpose as selecting "the exact phrase" option in Hotbot. The WebCrawler search only finds a few hundred hits. Some are the same as those found using HotBot, some are different. Different searching strategies and software algorithms make using more than one search engine a must for serious researchers.

The major search engines conveniently provide you with tips to help you get the most out of their searches. These include ways to use AND and OR to narrow down searches, and ways to use NOT to eliminate unwanted hits.

Each search engine also uses a slightly different approach to cataloging the Web, so at different sites your results might vary. Often, one search engine provides better results (more relevant hits) in your areas of interest; sometimes, the wise strategy is to provide the same input to several different engines. No one search engine does a perfect job all the time, so experience will dictate the one that's most valuable for you.

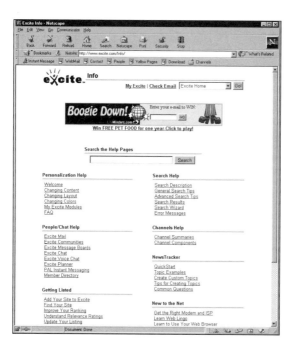

You'll find search tip pages like this at all the major search engine sites.

Quick Check

Let's review our searching strategies:

■ Visit one of the search engine sites;

■ Enter key words or phrases that best describe the search criteria;

■ Narrow the search if necessary by using options such as "all the words" or "the exact phrase." On some search engines, you may use the word "and" or the symbol "|" to indicate words that all must appear on a page;

■ Try using the same criteria with different search engines.

How Not to Come Down with a Virus

Downloading files from the Internet allows less responsible Net citizens to unleash onto your computer viruses, worms, and Trojan horses, all dangerous programs that fool you into thinking they're doing one thing while they're actually erasing your hard disk or performing some other undesirable task. Protection is your responsibility.

One way to reduce the risk of contracting a virus is to download software from reliable sites. Corporations such as Microsoft and Apple take care to make sure downloadable software is virus free. So do most institutions that provide software downloads as a public service (such as the Stanford University archives of Macintosh software). Be especially careful of programs you find on someone's home page. If you're not sure about safe download sources, ask around in a newsgroup (discussed shortly), talk to friends, or check with the information technology center on campus.

You can also buy and use a reliable virus program. Symantec and Dr. Solomon sell first-rate programs for the Mac and PC. You can update these programs right from the Internet so they'll detect the most current viruses. Most of the time, these programs can disinfect files/documents on your disk that contain viruses. Crude as it may sound, downloading programs from the Internet without using a virus check is like having unprotected sex with a stranger. While downloading software may not be life threatening, imagine the consequences if your entire hard disk, including all your course work and software, is totally obliterated. It won't leave you feeling very good.

part

1

The (E)mail Goes Through

Email was one of the first applications created for the Internet by its designers, who sought a method of communicating with each other directly from their keyboards. Your electronic Internet mailbox is to email what a post office box is to "snail mail" (the name Net citizens apply to ordinary, hand-delivered mail). This mailbox resides on the computer of your Internet Service Provider (ISP). That's the organization providing you with your Internet account. Most of the time your ISP will be your school; but, you may contract with one of the commercial providers, such as America Online, Mindspring, Microsoft Network, Earthlink, or AT&T. The Internet doesn't deliver a message to your door but instead leaves it in a conveniently accessible place (your mailbox) in the post office (the computer of your ISP), until you retrieve the mail using your combination (password).

If you currently have computer access to the Internet, your school or ISP assigned you a *user name* (also called a user id, account name, or account number). This user name may be your first name, your first initial and the first few characters of your last name, or some strange combination of numbers and letters only a computer could love. An email address is a combination of your user name and the unique address of the computer through which you access your email, like this:

```
username@computername.edu
```

The three letters after the dot, in this case "edu," identify the top level "domain." There are six common domain categories in use: edu (educational), com (commercial), org (organization), net (network), mil (military), and gov (government). The symbol "@"—called the "at" sign in typewriter days—serves two purposes: For computers, it provides a neat, clean separation between your user name and the computer name; for people, it makes Internet addresses more pronounceable. Your address is read: user name "at" computer name "dot" e-d-u. Suppose your Internet user name is "a4736g" and your ISP is Allyn & Bacon, the publisher of this book. Your email address might look like

```
a4736g@abacon.com
```

and you would tell people your email address is "ay-four-seven-three-six-gee at ay bacon dot com."

We Don't Just Handle Your Email, We're Also a Client

You use email with the aid of special programs called *mail clients*. As with search engines, mail clients have the same set of core features, but your access to these features varies with the type of program. On both the PC and the Mac, Netscape Communicator and Microsoft Internet Explorer give you access to mail clients while you're plugged into the Web. That way you can pick up and send mail while you're surfing the Web.

The basic email service functions are creating and sending mail, reading mail, replying to mail, and forwarding mail. First we'll examine the process of sending and reading mail, and then we'll discuss how to set up your programs so that your messages arrive safely.

Let's look at a typical mail client screen, in this case from Netscape Communicator 4.7. You reach this screen by choosing **Messenger** from under the **Communicator** menu. To send a message from scratch, choose the **New Msg** button to create a blank message form, which has fields for the recipient's address and the subject, and a window for the text of the message.

Fill in the recipient's address in the "To" field, just above the arrow. Use your own address. We'll send email to ourselves and use the same message to practice sending email and reading it as well; then we'll know if your messages come out as expected.

Click in the "Subject" field and enter a word or phrase that generally describes the topic of the message. Since we're doing this for the first time, let's type "Maiden Email Voyage."

Now click anywhere in the text window and enter your message. Let's say "Hi. Thanks for guiding me through sending my first email." You'll find that the mail client works here like a word processing program, which means you can insert and delete words and characters and highlight text.

Now click the **Send** button on the Navigation toolbar. You've just created and sent your first email message. In most systems, it takes a few seconds to a few minutes for a message to yourself to reach your mailbox, so you might want to take a short break before continuing. When you're ready to proceed, close the **Composition** window and click the **Get Msg** button.

part

1

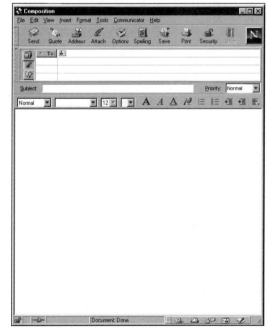

New message form, with fields for recipient's address and the subject, and a window for the text of the message.

What Goes Around Comes Around

Now let's grab hold of the message you just sent to yourself. When retrieving mail, most mail clients display a window showing the messages in your mailbox telling you how many new messages have been added.

If you've never used your email before, chances are your message window is empty, or contains only one or two messages (usually official messages from the ISP) besides the one you sent to yourself. The message to yourself should be accompanied by an indicator of some sort—a colored mark, the letter N—indicating it's a new message. In Netscape Communicator, as in other mail clients, you also get to see the date of the message, who sent it, and the information you entered in the subject line. The Subject field lets you scan your messages and determine which ones you want to look at first.

The summary of received messages tells you everything you need to know about a message except what's in it. Click anywhere in the line to see the contents in the message window. Click on the message from yourself and you'll see the contents of the message displayed in a window. The information at the top—To, From, Subject, and so forth—is called the *header*. Depending on your system, you may also see some cryptic lines with terms such as X-Mailer, received by, and id number. Most of the time, there's nothing in this part of the header of interest, so just skip over it for now.

Moving Forward

The contents, or text, of your message can be cut and pasted just like any other text document. If you and a classmate are working on a project together, your partner can write part of a paper and email it to you, and you can copy the text from your email message and paste it into your word processing program.

What if there are three partners in this project? One partner sends you a draft of the paper for you to review. You like it and want to send it on to your other partner. The **Forward** feature lets you send the message intact, so you don't have to cut and paste it into a new message window. To forward a message, highlight it in the **Inbox** (top) and click the **Forward** icon. Enter the recipient's address in the "To" field of the message window. Note that the subject of the message is "Fwd:" followed by the subject of the original message. Use the text window to add your comments ahead of the original message.

part

1

A Chance to Reply

Email is not a one-way message system. Let's walk through a reply to a message from a correspondent named Elliot. Highlight the message in your **Inbox** again and this time click on the **Reply** icon. Depending on which program you're using, you'll see that each line in the message is preceded by either a vertical bar or a right angle bracket (>).

Note the "To" and "Subject" fields are filled in automatically with the address of the sender and the original subject preceded by "Re:". In Internet terminology, the message has been *quoted*. The vertical bar or > is used to indicate lines not written by you but by someone else (in this case, the message's original author). Why bother? Because this feature allows you to reply without retyping the parts of the message you're responding to. Because your typing isn't quoted, your answers stand out from the original message. Netscape Communicator 4.7 adds some blank lines above and below your comments, a good practice for you if your mail client doesn't do this automatically.

Welcome to the Internet, Miss Manners

part

1

While we're on the subject of email, here are some *netiquette* (net etiquette) tips.

■ When you send email to someone, even someone who knows you well, all they have to look at are your words—there's no body language attached. That means there's no smile, no twinkle in the eye, no raised eyebrow; and especially, there's no tone of voice. What you write is open to interpretation and your recipient has nothing to guide him or her. You may understand the context of a remark, but will your reader? If you have any doubts about how your message will be interpreted, you might want to tack on an *emoticon* to your message. An emoticon is a face created out of keyboard characters. For example, there's the happy Smiley :-) (you have to look at it sideways . . . the parenthesis is its mouth), the frowning Smiley :-((Frownie?), the winking Smiley ;-), and so forth. Smileys are the body language of the Internet. Use them to put remarks in context. "Great," in response to a friend's suggestion means you like the idea. "Great :-(" changes the meaning to one of disappointment or sarcasm. (Want a complete list of emoticons? Try using "emoticon" as a key word for a Web search.)

■ Keep email messages on target. One of the benefits of email is its speed. Reading through lengthy messages leaves the reader wondering when you'll get to the point.

■ Email's speed carries with it a certain responsibility. Its ease of use and the way a messages seems to cry out for an answer both encourage quick responses, but quick doesn't necessarily mean thoughtful. Once you hit the **Send** icon, that message is gone. There's no recall button. Think before you write, lest you feel the wrath of the modern-day version of your parents' adage: Answer in haste, repent at leisure.

Keeping Things to Yourself

Here's another tip cum cautionary note, this one about Web security. Just as you take care to protect your wallet or purse while walking down a crowded street, it's only good practice to exercise caution with information you'd like to keep (relatively) private. Information you pass around the Internet is stored on, or passed along by, computers that are accessible to others. Although computer system administrators take great care to insure the security of this information, no scheme is completely infallible. Here are some security tips:

■ Exercise care when sending sensitive information such as credit card numbers, passwords, even telephone numbers and addresses in plain email. Your email message may pass through four or five computers en route to its destination, and at any of these points, it can be intercepted and read by someone other than the recipient.

■ Send personal information over the Web only if the page is secure. Web browsers automatically encrypt information on secure pages, and the information can only be unscrambled at the Web site that created the secure page. You can tell if a page is secure by checking the status bar at the bottom of your browser's window for an icon of a closed lock.

■ Remember that any files you store on your ISP's computer are accessible to unscrupulous hackers.

■ Protect your password. Many Web client programs, such as mail clients, have your password for you. That means anyone with physical access to your computer can read your email. With a few simple tools, someone can even steal your password. Never leave your password on a lab computer. (Make sure the **Remember Password** or **Save Password** box is unchecked in any application that asks for your password.)

The closed lock icon in the lower left-hand corner of your browser window indicates a "secure" Web page.

An Audience Far Wider Than You Imagine

Remember that the Web in particular and the Internet in general are communications mediums with a far-reaching audience, and placing information on the Internet is tantamount to publishing it. Certainly, the contents of any message or page you post become public information, but in a newsgroup (an electronic bulletin board), your email address also becomes public knowledge. On a Web page, posting a photo of your favorite music group can violate the photographer's copyright, just as if you published the image in a magazine. Use common sense about posting information you or someone else expects to remain private; and, remember, information on the Web can and will be read by people with different tastes and sensitivities. The Web tends to be self-censoring, so be prepared to handle feedback, both good and bad.

part

1

A Discussion of Lists

There's no reason you can't use email to create a discussion group. You pose a question, for example, by sending an email message to everyone in the group. Somebody answers and sends the answer to everyone else on the list, and so on.

At least, that's the theory.

In practice, this is what often happens. As people join and leave the group, you and the rest of your group are consumed with updating your lists, adding new names and deleting old ones. As new people join, their addresses may not make it onto the lists of all the members of the group, so different participants get different messages. The work of administering the lists becomes worse than any value anyone can get out of the group, and so it quickly dissolves.

Generally, you're better off letting the computer handle discussion group administration. A *list server* is a program for administering emailing lists. It automatically adds and deletes list members and handles the distribution of messages.

Thousands of mailing lists have already been formed by users with common interests. You may find mailing lists for celebrities, organizations, political interests, occupations, and hobbies. Your instructor may establish a mailing list for your course.

Groups come in several different flavors. Some are extremely active. You can receive as many as forty or more email messages a day. Other lists may send you a message a month. One-way lists, such as printed newsletters, do not distribute your reply to any other subscriber. Some lists distribute replies to everyone. These lists include mediated lists, in which an "editor" reviews each reply for suitability (relevance, tone, use of language) before distributing the message, and unmediated lists, in which each subscriber's response is automatically distributed to all the other subscribers with no restrictions except those dictated by decency

part

1

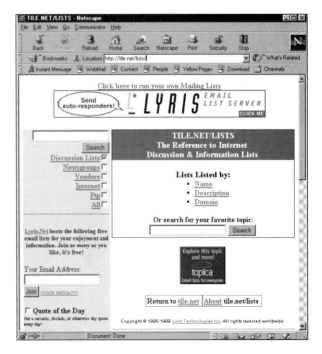

Tile.Net offfers shortcuts to working your way through the Internet's maze of discussion lists.

and common sense, though these qualities may not always be obvious from reading the messages.

Get on a List Online

You join in the discussion by subscribing to a list, which is as straightforward as sending email. You need to know only two items: the name of the list and the address of the list server program handling subscriptions. To join a list, send a **Subscribe** message to the list server address. The message is usually as simple as "subscribe," the name of the list, and your name (your real name, not your user name), all on one line. *And that's all.* This message will be read by a computer program that looks for these items only. At the very best, other comments in the message will be ignored. At the very worst, your entire message will be ignored, and so will you.

Within a few hours to a day after subscribing, the list server will automatically send you a confirmation email message, including instructions for sending messages, finding out information about the list and its members, and canceling your subscription. Save this message for future reference. That way, if you do decide to leave the list, you won't have to circulate a message to the members asking how to unsubscribe, and you won't have to wade through fifty replies all relaying the same information you received when you joined.

Soon after your confirmation message appears in your mailbox, and depending on the activity level of the list, you'll begin receiving email messages. New list subscribers customarily wait a while before joining the discussion. After all, you're electronically strolling into a room full of strangers; it's only fair to see what topics are being discussed before wading in with your own opinions. Otherwise, you're like the bore at the party who elbows his way into a conversation with "But enough about you, let's talk about me." You'll also want to avoid the faux pas of posting a long missive on a topic that subscribers spent the preceding three weeks thrashing out. Observe the list for a while, understand its tone and feel, what topics are of interest to others and what areas are taboo. Also, look for personalities. Who's the most vociferous? Who writes very little but responds thoughtfully? Who's the most flexible? The most rigid? Most of all, keep in mind that there are far more observers than participants. What you write may be read by 10 or 100 times more people than those whose names show up in the daily messages.

When you reply to a message, you reply to the list server address, not to the address of the sender (unless you intend for your communication to remain private). The list server program takes care of distributing

part

1

your message listwide. Use the address in the "Reply To" field of the message. Most mail clients automatically use this address when you select the **Reply** command. Some may ask if you want to use the reply address (say yes). Some lists will send a copy of your reply to you so you know your message is online. Others don't send the author a copy, relying on your faith in the infallibility of computers.

In the words of those famous late night television commercials, you can cancel your subscription at any time. Simply send a message to the address you used to subscribe (which you'll find on that confirmation message you saved for reference), with "unsubscribe," followed on the same line by the name of the list. For example, to leave a list named "WRITER-L," you would send:

```
unsubscribe WRITER-L
```

Even if you receive messages for a short while afterwards, have faith—they will disappear.

Waste Not, Want Not

List servers create an excellent forum for people with common interests to share their views; however, from the Internet standpoint, these lists are terribly wasteful. First of all, if there are one thousand subscribers to a list, every message must be copied one thousand times and distributed over the Internet. If there are forty replies a day, this one list creates forty thousand email messages. Ten such lists mean almost a half million messages, most of which are identical, flying around the Net.

Another wasteful aspect of list servers is the way in which messages are answered. The messages in your mailbox on any given day represent a combination of new topics and responses to previous messages. But where are these previous messages? If you saved them, they're in your email mailbox taking up disk space. If you haven't saved them, you have nothing to compare the response to. What if a particular message touches off a chain of responses, with subscribers referring not only to the source message but to responses as well? It sounds like the only safe strategy is to save every message from the list, a suggestion as absurd as it is impractical.

What we really need is something closer to a bulletin board than a mailing list. On a bulletin board, messages are posted once. Similar notices wind up clustered together. Everyone comes to the same place to read or post messages.

And Now the News(group)

The Internet equivalent of the bulletin board is the Usenet or newsgroup area. Usenet messages are copied only once for each ISP supporting the newsgroup. If there are one thousand students on your campus reading the same newsgroup message, there need only be one copy of the message stored on your school's computer.

Categorizing a World of Information

Newsgroups are categorized by topics, with topics broken down into subtopics and sub-subtopics. For example, you'll find newsgroups devoted to computers, hobbies, science, social issues, and "alternatives." Newsgroups in this last category cover a wide range of topics that may not appeal to the mainstream. Also in this category are beginning newsgroups.

Usenet names are amalgams of their topics and subtopics, separated by dots. If you were interested in a newsgroup dealing with, say, music, you might start with rec.music and move down to rec.music.radiohead, or rec.music.techno, and so forth. The naming scheme allows you to zero in on a topic of interest.

part

1

Getting into the News(group) Business

Most of the work of reading, responding to, and posting messages is handled by a news reader client program, accessible through both Netscape Communicator and Microsoft Internet Explorer. You can not only surf the Web and handle your mail via your browser, but you can also drop into your favorite newsgroups virtually all in one operation.

Let's drop into a newsgroup. To reach groups via Netscape Communicator 4.7, go to the Communicator menu bar and select **Newsgroups.** Then, from the File menu, select **Subscribe.** A dialogue box will open that displays a list of available groups.

To subscribe to a newsgroup—that is, to tell your news reader you want to be kept up-to-date on the messages posted to a particular group—highlight the group of interest and click on **Subscribe.** Alternately, you can click in the Subscribe column to the right of the group name. The check mark in the Subscribe column means you're "in."Now, click **OK.**

The message center in Netscape Communicator displays a list of newsgroups on your subscription list. Double click on the one of current interest and your reader presents you with a list of messages posted on the group's bulletin board. Double click on a message to open its contents in a window.

Often, messages contain "Re:" in their subject lines, indicating a response to a previous message (the letters stand for "Regarding"). Many news readers maintain a *thread* for you. Threads are chains of messages and all responses to that message. These readers give you the option to read messages chronologically or to read a message followed by its responses.

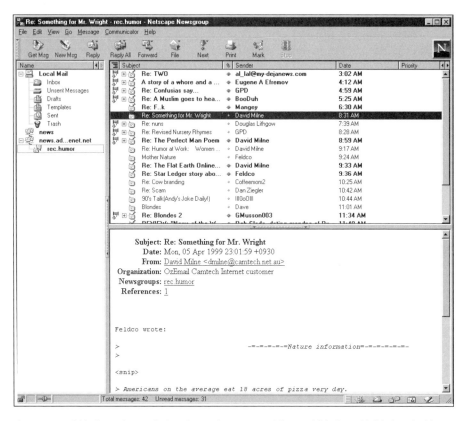

The top part of this figure shows a listing of posted messages. While not visible from this black and white reproduction, a red indicator in the Subject column marks unread messages. Double-clicking on a message opens its contents into a window shown in the bottom part of this figure. You can reply to this message via the Reply icon, or get the next message using the Next icon.

When you subscribe to a newsgroup, your news reader will also keep track of the messages you've read so that it can present you with the newest (unread) ones. While older messages are still available to you, this feature guarantees that you stay up-to-date without any record keeping on your part. Subscribing to a newsgroup is free, and the subscription information resides on your computer.

Newsgroups have no way of knowing who their subscribers are, and the same caveat that applies to bookmarks applies to newsgroups. Information about your subscriptions resides physically on the personal computer you're using. If you switch computers, as in a lab, your subscription information and history of read messages are beyond your reach.

Welcome to the Internet, Miss Manners—Again

As with list servers, hang out for a while, or *lurk,* to familiarize yourself with the style, tone, and content of newsgroup messages. As you probably surmised from the names of the groups, their topics of discussion are quite narrow. One of the no-nos of newsgroups is posting messages on subjects outside the focus of the group. Posting off-topic messages, especially lengthy ones, is an excellent way to attract a flaming.

A *flame* is a brutally debasing message from one user to another. Flames are designed to hurt and offend, and often the target of the flame feels compelled to respond in kind to protect his or her self-esteem. This leads to a *flame war,* as other users take sides and wade in with flames of their own. If you find yourself the target of a flame, your best strategy is to ignore it. As with a campfire, if no one tends to the flames, they soon die out.

As mentioned earlier, posting messages to newsgroups is a modern form of publishing, and a publisher assumes certain responsibilities. You have a duty to keep your messages short and to the point. Many newsgroup visitors connect to the Internet via modems. Downloading a day's worth of long postings, especially uninteresting ones, is annoying and frustrating. Similarly, don't post the same message to multiple, related newsgroups. This is called *cross posting,* and it's a peeve of Net citizens who check into these groups. If you've ever flipped the television from channel to channel during a commercial break only to encounter the same commercial (an advertising practice called *roadblocking*), you can imagine how annoying it is to drop in on several newsgroups only to find the same messages posted to each one.

part

1

With the huge potential audience newsgroups offer, you might think you've found an excellent medium for advertising goods or services. After all, posting a few messages appears analogous to running classified ads in newspapers, only here the cost is free. There's a name for these kinds of messages—*spam*. Spam is the junk mail of the Internet, and the practice of spamming is a surefire way to attract flames. The best advice for handling spam? Don't answer it. Not only does an answer encourage the spammer, but he or she will also undoubtedly put your email address on a list and sell it to other spammers, who will flood your online mailbox with their junk.

Above all, be considerate of others. Treat them the way you'd like to be treated. Do you enjoy having your grammar or word choices corrected in front of the whole world? Do you feel comfortable when someone calls you stupid in public? Do you appreciate having your religion, ethnicity, heritage, or gender belittled in front of an audience? Respect the rights and feelings of others, if not out of simple decency then out of the sanctions your ISP may impose. Although you have every right to express an unpopular opinion or to take issue with the postings of others, most ISPs have regulations about the kinds of messages one can send via their facilities. Obscenities, threats, and spam may, at a minimum, result in your losing your Internet access privileges.

part

1

Give Your Web Browser Some Personality—Yours

Before accessing email and newsgroup functions, you need to set up or personalize your browser. If you always work on the same personal computer, this is a one-time operation that takes only a few minutes. In it, you tell your browser where to find essential computer servers, along with personal information the Internet needs to move messages for you.

■ *Step 1:*   Open the **Preferences** menu in Netscape or the **Internet Options** in Internet Explorer. In Netscape Communicator the Preferences menu is located under the **Edit** menu; in Microsoft Internet Explorer the Internet Options can be found under the **View** menu.

■ *Step 2:*   Tell the browser who you are and where to find your mail servers. Your Reply To address is typically the same as your email address, though if you have an email alias you can use it here. Your ISP will provide the server names and addresses.

SMTP handles your outgoing messages, while the POP3 server routes incoming mail. Often, but not always, these server names are the same.

■ *Step 3:* Tell the browser where to find your news server. Your ISP will furnish the name of the server. Note that in Microsoft Internet Explorer, you specify a helper application to read the news. Now that most computers come with browsers already loaded onto the hard disk, you'll find that these helper applications are already set up for you.

■ *Step 4:* Set your home page. For convenience, you may want your browser to start by fetching a particular page, such as your favorite search site. Or you might want to begin at your school library's home page. Enter the URL for this starting page in the home page address field. Both Netscape and Microsoft offer the option of no home page when you start up. In that case, you get a blank browser window.

Operating systems such as Mac OS 8 or 9 and Microsoft Windows 95, 98, and 2000 offer automated help in setting up your browsers for Web, mail, and newsgroup operation. You need to know the names of the servers mentioned above, along with your user name and other details, such as the address of the domain name server (DNS) of your ISP. You should receive all this information when you open your Internet account. If not, ask for it.

part

1

Critical Evaluation

Where Seeing Is Not Always Believing

Typical research resources, such as journal articles, books, and other scholarly works, are reviewed by a panel of experts before being published. At the very least, any reputable publisher takes care to assure that the author is who he or she claims to be and that the work being published represents a reasoned and informed point of view. When anyone can post anything in a Web site or to a newsgroup, the burden of assessing the relevance and accuracy of what you read falls to you. Rumors quickly grow into facts on the Internet simply because stories can spread so rapidly that the "news" seems to be everywhere. Because the Internet leaves few tracks, in no time it's impossible to tell whether you are reading independent stories or the merely same story that's been around the world two or three times. Gathering information on the Internet may be quick, but verifying the quality of information requires a serious commitment.

Approach researching via the Internet with confidence, however, and not with trepidation. You'll find it an excellent workout for your critical evaluation skills; no matter what career you pursue, employers value an employee who can think critically and independently. Critical thinking is also the basis of problem solving, another ability highly valued by the business community. So, as you research your academic projects, be assured that you're simultaneously developing lifelong expertise.

It's Okay to Be Critical of Others

The first tip for successful researching on the Internet is to always consider your source. A Web site's URL often alerts you to the sponsor of the site. CNN or MSNBC are established news organizations, and you can give the information you find at their sites the same weight you would give to their cablecasts. Likewise, major newspapers operate Web sites with articles reprinted from their daily editions or expanded stories written expressly for the Internet. On the other hand, if you're unfamiliar with the source, treat the information the way you would any new data. Look for specifics—"66 percent of all voters" as opposed to "most voters"—and for information that can be verified—a cited report in another medium or information accessible through a Web site hosted by a credible sponsor—as opposed to generalities or unverifiable claims. Look for independent paths to the same information. This can involve careful use of search engines or visits to newsgroups with both similar and opposing viewpoints. Make sure that the "independent" information you find is truly independent. In newsgroups don't discount the possibility of multiple postings, or that a posting in one group is nothing more than a quotation from a posting in another. Ways to verify independent paths include following sources (if any) back to their origins, contacting the person posting a message and asking for clarification, or checking other media for verification.

In many cases, you can use your intuition and common sense to raise your comfort level about the soundness of the information. With both list servers and newsgroups, it's possible to lurk for a while to develop a feeling for the authors of various postings. Who seems the most authoritarian, and who seems to be "speaking" from emotion or bias? Who seems to know what he or she is talking about on a regular basis? Do these people cite their sources of information (a job or affiliation perhaps)? Do they have a history of thoughtful, insightful postings, or do their postings typically contain generalities, unjustifiable claims, or flames? On Web sites, where the information feels more anonymous, there are also clues you can use to test for authenticity. Verify who's hosting the Web site. If the host or domain name is unfamiliar to you, perhaps a search engine can help you locate more information. Measure the tone and style of the writing at the site. Does it seem consistent with the education level and knowledge base necessary to write intelligently about the subject?

When offering an unorthodox point of view, good authors supply facts, figures, and quotes to buttress their positions, expecting readers to be skeptical of their claims. Knowledgeable authors on the Internet follow these same commonsense guidelines. Be suspicious of authors who expect you to agree with their points of view simply because they've published them on the Internet. In one-on-one encounters, you frequently judge the authority and knowledge of the speaker using criteria you'd be hard pressed to explain. Use your sense of intuition on the Internet, too.

As a researcher (and as a human being), the job of critical thinking requires a combination of healthy skepticism and rabid curiosity. Newsgroups and Web sites tend to focus narrowly on single issues (newsgroups more so than Web sites). Don't expect to find a torrent of opposing views on newsgroup postings; their very nature and reason for existence dampens free-ranging discussions. A newsgroup on *The X-Files* might argue about whether extraterrestrials exist but not whether the program is the premier television show on the air today. Such a discussion would run counter to the purposes of the newsgroup and would be a violation of netiquette. Anyone posting such a message would be flamed, embarrassed, ignored, or otherwise driven away. Your research responsibilities include searching for opposing views by visiting a variety of newsgroups and Web sites. A help here is to fall back on the familiar questions of journalism: who, what, when, where, and why.

part

1

- **Who** else might speak knowledgeably on this subject? Enter that person's name into a search engine. You might be surprised to find whose work is represented on the Web. (For fun, one of the authors entered the name of a rock-and-roll New York radio disk jockey into MetaCrawler and was amazed to find several pages devoted to the DJ, including sound clips of broadcasts dating back to the sixties, along with a history of his theme song.)
- **What** event might shed more information on your topic? Is there a group or organization that represents your topic? Do they hold an

annual conference? Are synopses of presentations posted on the sponsoring organization's Web site?

- ■ **When** do events happen? Annual meetings or seasonal occurrences can help you isolate newsgroup postings of interest.

- ■ **Where** might you find this information? If you're searching for information on wines, for example, check to see if major wine-producing regions, such as the Napa Valley in California or the Rhine Valley in Germany, sponsor Web sites. These may point you to organizations or information that don't show up in other searches. Remember, Web search engines are fallible; they don't find every site you need.

- ■ **Why** is the information you're searching for important? The answer to this question can lead you to related fields. New drugs, for example, are important not only to victims of diseases but to drug companies and the FDA as well.

part

1

Approach assertions you read from a skeptic's point of view. See if they stand up to critical evaluation or if you're merely emotionally attached to them. Imagine "What if . . . ?" or "What about . . . ?" scenarios that may disprove or at least call into question what you're reading. Try following each assertion you pull from the Internet with the phrase, "On the other hand. . . ." Because you can't leave the sentence hanging, you'll be forced to finish it, and this will help get you into the habit of critically examining information.

These are, of course, the same techniques critical thinkers have employed for centuries, only now you are equipped with more powerful search tools than past researchers may have ever imagined. In the time it took your antecedents to formulate their questions, you can search dozens of potential information sources. You belong to the first generation of college students to enjoy both quantity and quality in its research, along with a wider perspective on issues and the ability to form personal opinions after reasoning from a much wider knowledge base. Certainly, the potential exists for the Internet to grind out a generation of intellectual robots, "thinkers" who don't think but who regurgitate information from many sources. Technology always has its good and bad aspects. However, we also have the potential to become some of the most well-informed thinkers in the history of the world, thinkers who are not only articulate but confident that their opinions have been distilled from a range of views, processed by their own personalities, beliefs, and biases. This is one of the aspects of the Internet that makes this era such an exciting combination of humanism and technology.

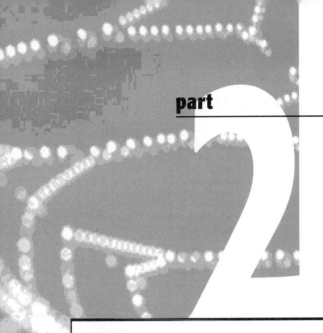

part

Psychology Activities

Overview

Careers in Psychology

Go to **http://www.psychwww.com/.** The resources on this page focus on: (1) careers in psychology at the bachelor's, master's, and doctoral level and (2) academic information about psychology at the bachelor's and graduate levels.

Which area of psychology did you find most interesting?

_____

_____

_____

Which career path would you choose for the bachelor's, master's, and doctoral level. Explain you rational.

_____

_____

_____

The Two Major Professional Psychology Organizations

Until recently there has been only one major professional organization for psychologists, the American Psychological Association (APA), **http://www.apa.org/.** In 1988, a second organization was formed. The American Psychological Society (APS) **http://www. psychologicalscience.org** is quite different in scope and purpose.

Your task is to compare and contrast the two professional organizations. What do they have in common and where do they differ? In order to accomplish this task you will have to spend some time exploring at each site. Take your time to understand the two major professional organizations in psychology.

What is the stated purpose of APA?

_____

_____

_____

part

2

What is the stated purpose of APS?

_____

_____

_____

What do APA and APS have in common?

_____

_____

_____

What are the advantages and disadvantages joining APA?

_____

_____

_____

What are the advantages and disadvantages joining APS?

_____

_____

_____

Which organization would you join and why?

_____

_____

_____

Happy Birthday?

Go to **http://www.cwu.edu/~warren/calendar/datepick.html,** select
your birthday, and see what happened in the history of psychology
that day.

part

2

What was the most significant event that happened on your birthday?
Explain why:

_____

_____

_____

_____

Go for the Money

You have finally graduated from college and are working for a famous
research group. This is a great place to work and the pay is fantastic, so
you are content with your new position. But there is one small catch.
You have to write a grant to receive funding in order to keep your job.
This project is designed so that you can utilize the Internet to find agen-
cies for funding opportunities. Start at **http://www.nimh.nih.gov/** for
your search.

Your research topic in psychology for the grant _____

_____

Site I found that is a good opportunity for my grant:

http://_____

Name _____

Site I found that is a good opportunity for my grant:

http://_____

Name _____

Site I found that is a good opportunity for my grant:

http://_____

Name _____

Site I found that is a good opportunity for my grant:

http://_____

Name _____

part

2

Site I found that is a good opportunity for my grant:

http://_____

Name _____

Site I found that is a good opportunity for my grant:

http://_____

Name _____

Site I found that is a good opportunity for my grant:

http://_____

Name _____

Site I found that is a good opportunity for my grant:

http://_____

Name _____

Site I found that is a good opportunity for my grant:

http://_____

Name _____

Site I found that is a good opportunity for my grant:

http://_____

Name _____

Biological Basis of Behavior

Hello Dolly *et al*

Science and humankind have entered a new era with the discovery of the ability to clone large mammals. Quite recently human DNA has been inserted in a cloned sheep, adding to the interest in this topic. Go to **http://whyfiles.news.wisc.edu/034clone/main1.html** and explore the site. This may take some time, but it will allow you to answer some interesting questions. There are no right or wrong answers to these questions, but take the time to think and then write about the following:

Should we attempt to clone a human?

_____

_____

_____

part

2

What are the ethical consideration of cloning animals and humans?

_____

_____

_____

Should the U.S. government stop funding basic research into cloning as proposed by President Clinton?

_____

_____

_____

Would you consider cloning yourself?

_____

_____

_____

Sensation and Perception

Exploratorium

Go to **http://www.exploratorium.edu/imagery/exhibits.html** and explore three different kinds of illusions. Most of these exhibits are electronic versions from the museum floor; a few are unique.

Which of the many types of illusions do you find the most interesting?

_____

_____

_____

part

2

Which specific illusion was the most interesting and why?

_____

_____

_____

After exploring this page do you think seeing is believing?

_____

_____

_____

States of Consciousness

Parapsychology: Real or Sham

What is parapsychology? Answer this question before going to **http://moebius.psy.ed.ac.uk/gr_index.html.**

_____

_____

_____

Now go to the site and search for the answer to the question What is parapsychology? Is the answer different than your earlier answer? If so, how?

_____

_____

_____

Is the study of parapsychology a legitimate area of inquiry for psychology?

_____

_____

_____

Is parapsychology real or a sham?

_____

part

2

_____

_____

Memory and Learning

Enhancing Your Memory

http://www.psychwww.com/mtsite/memory.html. This site contains many links to sites that are intended to improve your memory. All students of psychology, from the entering freshperson to the full professor, are interested in improving their memory. Go to this site and pick three topics of interest. Follow the instructions and proceed through the exercise.

Which topics did you choose?

1. _____

2. _____

3. _____

Which of the topics was the most interesting?

_____

_____

_____

Which of the topics was the most useful to you as a student of psychology and why?

_____

_____

_____

part 2 Cognition and Intelligence

What is Your IQ? Traditional and Nontraditional

Go to **http://www.geocities.com/CapitolHill/1641/iqown.html.** Here you will find a traditional IQ tests. Take the one that interests you the most.

Which test did you take? _____

How did you do? Were you better or worse than you thought you would be prior to taking this test?

_____

_____

_____

What could you do to improve your score on the specific test?

_____

_____

_____

Did you feel this test was a valid test of your IQ? If not, why not?

_____

_____

_____

Now go to **http://www.2h.com/Tests/iqalt.phtml.** This site tests alternative IQ, with some humorous tests that include IQ's for your romance, jewelry, and garbage IQ's.

Which test did you like the best? Which did you like the least?

_____

_____

_____

Which IQ test appeared to be the most valid? Explain your answer.

part

2

_____

_____

_____

Motivation and Emotion

Eating Disorders: Killers

Many of us have either observed the behavior of others or our own behavior and wondered, "Do I have an eating disorder?" Go to **http://site.health-center.com/brain/eatingdisorder/default.htm** and go to several links that might answer this question.

What is anorexia nervosa and how is it defined?

_____

_____

_____

What is bulimia and how is it defined?

_____

_____

_____

What course of action should you take if you know someone with these behaviors, whether a friend or yourself?

_____

_____

_____

part

2

Child and Adolescent Development

You're Having a Baby

Go to **http://www.efn.org/~djz/birth/birthindex.html.** This page has many diverse topics on very early development in humans. Pick a topic that you know little about and explore the links.

Topic _____

What new information did you discover?

_____

_____

_____

If you are not now a parent, how will this information affect how you approach parenthood?

_____

_____

_____

Adult Development and Aging

The Graying of America

Got to **http://www.aoa.dhhs.gov/.** What are the three major problems or concerns you could expect to face as a parent or grand parent ages? The information on this URL will guide you to specific concerns for individuals who are aging.

1. _____

   _____

   _____

2. _____

   _____

   _____

part

2

3. _____

   _____

   _____

By the time you reach retirement, which of these three problem areas mentioned above will no longer be a concern because of discoveries in the sciences or psychology? Which of these areas will not be a problem to you and why?

_____

_____

_____

Personality

Do You Have a Type A Personality?

Go to **http://www.queendom.com/typea2.html,** an online personality test containing seventeen items which attempts to differentiate between A- and B-type personalities.

Does this test seem valid? Is it really measuring Type A personality?

_____

_____

_____

If you have a Type A personality as measured in this test, what measures would you take to change your behaviors and thus your responses on the test?

_____

_____

_____

If you did not have an Type A personality, describe a friend's behaviors and discuss how you would advise this person to change his or her behaviors.

_____

_____

_____

Comparing Freud and Jung

Two of the major figures in psychology in the first half of this century are Sigmund Freud and Carl Jung. Both were concerned with personality theories and abnormal behavior. Go to **http://www.cgjung.com/cgjung/**

for Jung and **http://plaza.interport.net/nypsan/** for Freud. Use these sites as starting points to explore the philosophy and theories of both psychologists.

How did Freud and Jung differ in their approach to personality?

_____

_____

_____

How did Freud and Jung agree in their approach to personality?

_____

_____

_____

What aspect of each psychologist's theories did you find most interesting?

_____

_____

_____

part

2

Stress and Health

Go Ask Alice

Go to **http://www.goaskalice.columbia.edu/.** This site contains the Health Education and Wellness program of the Columbia University Health Service. This site is committed to helping individual's make choices that will contribute to your personal health and happiness.

  Be warned that this site can contain very graphic descriptions of sexual activity and advice about sexual activity that some individuals may find disturbing.

What was the most interesting location you visited at this site?

_____

_____

_____

What new information did you learn from this site?

_____

_____

_____

The Longevity Game

How long will you live? This question has been considered since individuals started thinking. You have information about your parents' and grandparents' longevity. Is their longevity a good indicator of your longevity or are other factors as important? The Longevity Game allows you to assess your own probabilities of reaching a specific age based on your life style. Go to **http://www.northwesternmutual.com/games/longevity/** and proceed with the questions.

How long are you projected to live? _____

Are you shocked, happy or surprised by the calculated number? Explain

_____

_____

_____

What factors are the most positive? What factors are the most negative?

_____

_____

_____

part
2

What life style factors could you change to increase your estimated longevity?

_____

_____

_____

Return to the game and change some of the life style factors for which you received the largest negative numbers on the summary table. How much did these life style changes affect your estimated life span?

_____

_____

_____

Are these life style changes worth the effort involved in making them in order to add years to your longevity?

_____

_____

_____

part
2

Psychological Disorders and Treatment

Who is Crazy?

We have all known individuals (friends) that have strange or bizarre behaviors either in real life or in the media (films and TV). Choose three tests from **http://www.med.nyu.edu/Psych/itp.html** and take a test using the behaviors you have noted in these individuals. Are these individuals diagnosable using these tests? Or are they just eccentric?

Test Name _____

Results test # 1

_____

_____

_____

Results test # 2

_____

_____

_____

Results test # 3

_____

_____

_____

Choosing a Psychologist

Many times individuals (friends and family) feel that they are in need of professional help. Go to **http://helping.apa.org/brochure/index.html** to help answer the question, "Do I need a psychologist?"

What was the most important information that you discovered at this site?

_____

_____

_____

Has this site increased or decreased your perceived need to find a psychologist for a friend or family member?

_____

_____

_____

Social Psychology

Social Influence

Go to **http://www.influenceatwork.com/**. This web site is devoted to social influence—the modern, scientific study of persuasion, compliance, and propaganda.

What information at this site did you find most interesting?

_____

_____

_____

What techniques did you learn from this site to help yourself guard against social influence pressures?

part

2

_____

_____

_____

Exploring Social Psychology

Social psychology is a very large area of psychology. Go to **http://cac.psu.edu/~arm3/social.html** and explore one resource for social psychology and one social psychology program. Choose the area that most interests you and a school that you might like to attend, either as an undergraduate or graduate student.

Which resource site did you choose? _____

What was the most interesting aspect of this site?

_____

_____

_____

Which program did you choose?

_____

_____

_____

Would you still like to attend this school now that you have explored its social psychology program?

_____

_____

_____

What were the most positive and negative factors you discovered at the program?

_____

_____

_____

part
2

Applied Psychology

What Is Forensic Psychology?

Go to **http://forensic.to/forensic.html.** Zeno's Forensic Page is a large site with many links in the area of forensic psychology.

After exploring this site what is you definition of Forensic Psychology?

_____

_____

_____

What unique material did you discover at this site?

_____

_____

_____

After viewing this site would you consider Forensic Psychology as a career? Explain.

_____

_____

_____

What Is Sports Psychology?

Go to **http://spot.colorado.edu/~collinsj/.** Search the links and organization in order to develop a definition of sports psychology.

part

2

What is your definition of sports psychology?

_____

_____

_____

Can sports psychology enhance the performance of athletes?

_____

_____

_____

Would you like to consider sports psychology as a career? If not, why not? If is yes, explain.

_____

_____

_____

Skills on the Internet

Scavenger Hunt on the Internet

This exercise is designed to test your skills on the Internet. I have chosen a number of questions related to the long running TV series *Star Trek*. Your parents were amazed when the original *Star Trek* aired. Now the show has evolved into several new series with new plots and characters. Your task is to use the Internet to answer the following questions.

I have not supplied any URLs as starting points, so you will have to begin with a search engine. They can be found at your service provider's home page or at these two major sites: **http://www.altavista.com/,** or **http://www.yahoo.com/.**

Some of these questions are easy; others may have no real answer. Good luck.

part

2

1. What was the studio that produced the original series?

   _____

2. When was the first "Star Trek" aired and what was the title?

   _____

   _____

3. How did *Voyager* get to the Delta quadrant?   _____

   _____

4. What does the "T" in James T. Kirk stand for?   _____

   _____

5. Was Scotty really Scottish? What university did he graduate from?

   _____

6. What was the original starship *Enterprise*'s ID number?

   _____

7. Where and when was Data activated?   _____

   _____

8. What was Data's brother's name? Was the brother older or younger?

   _____

9. Who built Deep Space 9 and why was it abandoned?

   _____

10. When was the first episode of _Voyager_ aired?   _____

    _____

11. Where is the Klingon home world? _____

    _____

12. How many hosts has DAX shared? _____

    _____

Web Resources for Psychology

Overview

part
2

Psychology Departments on the Web

`http://www.psychwww.com/resource/deptlist.htm`

This very extensive listing of all psychology departments on the Internet is a must for any student making decision about which program to attend.

Careers in psychology

`http://www.psychwww.com/careers/index.htm`

The resources on this page focus on: (1) careers in psychology at the bachelor's, master's, and doctoral level and (2) academic information about psychology at the bachelor's and graduate levels.

Experimental and Correlational Research

`http://www.indiana.edu/~gasser/experiments.html`

Causal relationships and experimental research and definitions of terms are discussed at this site.

Ethics in Research

http://methods.fullerton.edu/chapter3.html

This site contains ethics codes and research links on the Internet.

Gallup Polls

http://www.gallup.com/

This site features public releases, special reports on key social and business-related issues, and Gallup Polls, a major source for public opinion data since 1935.

Educational Testing Service

http://www.ets.org/

This is the Educational Testing Service home page, with information for parents and students, educator-researchers and policymakers.

part
2

Code of Conduct

http://www.apa.org/ethics/code.html

This American Psychological Association site deals with ethical principles of psychologists and defines the code of conduct.

Statistics on the Web

http://www.spss.com/StatsWeb/

Statistics on the World Wide Web may be found at this site, along with many links to other sites.

The Lifschitz Psychology Museum

http://www.netaxs.com/people/aca3/LPM.HTM

This is the World's First Virtual Museum of Psychology, established February 1, 1996.

The Mind Body Problem

http://serendip.brynmawr.edu/Mind/Table.html

This site was derived for the *Exhibition of Books from the Collections of the National Library of Medicine,* held in honor of the *Centennial Celebration of the American Psychological Association,* August 7 to December 15, 1992

Statistic Glossary

http://www.cas.lancs.ac.uk/glossary_v1.1/main.html

This comprehensive site defines and gives examples of statistical concepts and terms.

William James

http://serendip.brynmawr.edu/Mind/James.html

This site contains a history of William James, the man who helped advance the Mind/Body Problem and the psychologist considered by many to be one of the most influential in history.

part

2

Psychological Research on the Net

http://psych.hanover.edu/APS/exponnet.html

Links to known experiments on the Internet that are psychologically related are organized by general topic areas with the topic areas listed alphabetically.

Major Areas of Psychology

http://www.gasou.edu/psychweb/tipsheet/specialt.htm

Explanations of ten different specialty areas in psychology—clinical, counseling, developmental, educational, experimental, health, industrial/organizational, physiological, school, and social psychology—are found at this site.

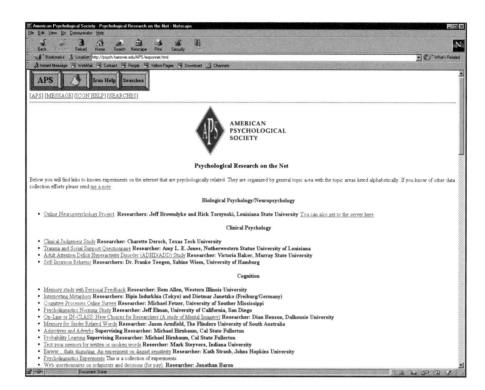

Experimental Psychology

http://www.york.ac.uk/depts/psych/www/etc/
whatispsych.html

A description of experimental psychology, this site also deals with the
common misconceptions of psychology.

Careers in Psychology

http://www.rider.edu/users/suler/gradschl.html

This site offers a detailed discussion of what one can do with a
degree in psychology, the types of subfields, and how to get into
graduate school.

Today in the History of Psychology

http://www.cwu.edu/~warren/today.html

This interactive site allows the user to pick a date and see what happened in psychology on that date.

Usenet Newsgroups

`http://www-psych.stanford.edu/cogsci/usenet.html`

This is a large set of links to news groups.

Biological Basis of Behavior

Basic Neural Processes Tutorials

`http://psych.hanover.edu/Krantz/neurotut.html`

This is a short tutorial of the basics of neural processing.

Neuroscience on the Internet

`http://www.neuroguide.com/index4.html#live`

This searchable database includes many links.

Neuropsychology Central

`http://www.neuropsychologycentral.com/`

An extremely large and diverse site that contains links to many other sites, including assessment, treatment, organizations, image sites and medical consideration, this is one of the most complete sites on the Net. It even includes music.

Neurotransmission

`http://www.csuchico.edu/psy/BioPsych/`
`neurotransmission.html`

A tutorial of the basics of neurotransmission, including the synapse and parts of the neuron can be accessed at this site.

Brain Imaging

`http://www.bic.mni.mcgill.ca/demos/`

These are interesting examples of brain imaging techniques. The brain imaging demos at this site require a graphics browser.

Neuroscience

http://faculty.washington.edu/chudler/ehceduc.html

This extremely detailed site consists of links for education and is large enough to spend several days exploring. It is must for anyone interested in the neuroscience.

Genetics

http://www.med.jhu.edu/Greenberg.Center/
tutorial.htm#basics

This site offers a rather in-depth discussion of genetics and inheritance.

The Whole Brain Atlas

http://www.med.harvard.edu/AANLIB/home.html

part
2

A complete reference to the brain, this site has information, images, and QuickTime movies all related to the brain. Included is a discussion on the pathology of Alzheimer's disease.

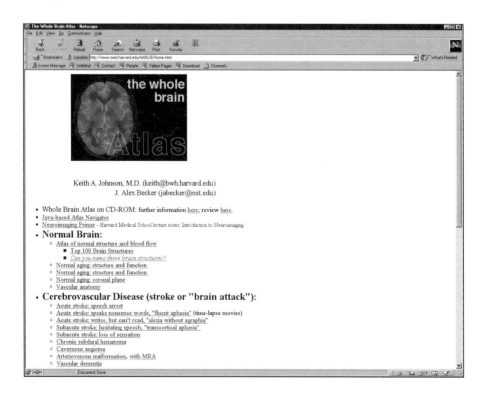

The Visible Human Project

http://www.nlm.nih.gov/research/visible/
visible_human.html

The Visible Human Project is creating complete, anatomically detailed, three-dimensional representations of the male and female human bodies.

Human Brain Project

http://www-hbp.scripps.edu/

This is the home page of Human Brain Project in the UK.

Human Genome Project

http://www.ornl.gov/TechResources/Human_Genome/
home.html

This home page is maintained by the Human Genome Management Information System (HGMIS) for the U.S. Department of Energy Human Genome Program. Explore this site for material about the history, progress, research, and resources of the Human Genome Project.

part
2

Neuroscience

http://neuro.med.cornell.edu/VL/

This World-Wide Web Virtual Library is supported by The Department of Neurology and Neuroscience at Cornell University Medical College.

Cognitive-Neuroscience Resources

http://www-cgi.cs.cmu.edu/afs/cs/project/cnbc/other/
other-neuro.html

Listings of cognitive-neuroscience resources sites are available here.

McConnell Brain Imaging Center

http://www.bic.mni.mcgill.ca/

The McConnell Brain Imaging Center (BIC) is one of the largest scientific communities in North America dedicated solely to research imaging of the human brain.

Split Brain

http://ezinfo.ucs.indiana.edu/~pietsch/
split-brain.html

Detailed discussion of the split brain operations and its effects are presented from a research view point.

Sensation and Perception

Kinesthetic Child

http://www.latitudes.org/learn01.html

The Fine Line Between ADHD and Kinesthetic Learners is discussed at this site.

Subliminal Persuasion

http://www.yahoo.com/Science/Cognitive_Science/
Unconscious_Cognition/Subliminal_Perception/

A discussion of backward masking, hypnosis, and subliminal advertising can be found at this site.

Auditory Perception

http://neuro.bio.tu-darmstadt.de/langner/
langner_e.html

Auditory research links are available at this site.

Exploratorium

http://www.exploratorium.edu/imagery/
exhibits.html

This site contains digital versions of Exploratorium exhibits. It is important understand that these versions in most cases are not adequate replacements for the real experiences that you will have if you are able to visit the Exploratorium in San Francisco. Most of these exhibits are electronic versions from the museum floor; a few are unique.

Historical Origins of Color Vision Research

```
http://kiptron.psyc.virginia.edu/steve_boker/
ColorVision2/node3.html
```

This site contains links to important individuals in the history of color vision research.

Illusionworks

```
http://www.illusionworks.com/
```

This is one the most comprehensive collections of optical and sensory illusions on the Internet.

Perception of Facial Aging Laboratory.

```
http://psych.st-and.ac.uk:8080/research/
perception_lab/
```

An interactive site that discusses research of facial aging perception, the site allows users to look live on-line into the research laboratory and

part

2

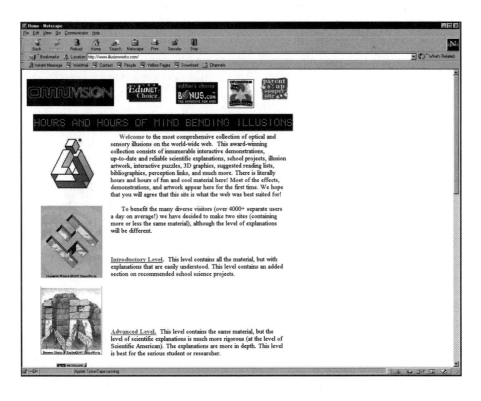

watch the researchers at work. This site is in the UK so the time difference is considerable.

Kubovy Perception Lab University of Virginia Department of Psychology

http://minerva.acc.virginia.edu/~mklab/

This site is a working laboratory studying topics like Gestalt detection, symmetry perception, picture perception, skin reading, and rhythm and time perception.

University of California at Santa Cruz Perceptual Science Laboratory

http://mambo.ucsc.edu/

The Perceptual Science Laboratory is engaged in a variety of experimental and theoretical inquiries in perception and cognition. A major research area concerns speech perception by ear, eye, and facial animation.

Vision Research WWW Servers

http://www.socsci.uci.edu/cogsci/vision.html

All there is to know about visual perception is contained in these links, from university laboratories to organizations concerned with visual perception.

Auditory Perception

http://www.music.mcgill.ca/auditory/Auditory.html

A multimedia presentation of selected topics in auditory perception, including auditory demonstrations, discussion, and experiments in perception

The Joy of Visual Perception: A Web Book

http://www.yorku.ca/research/vision/eye/

This is an interactive book with links.

part

2

International Symposium on Olfaction and Taste

http://www.psychology.sdsu.edu/ISOT/

Details of a convention on olfaction and taste can be found at this site.

Cow Eye Dissection

http://www.exploratorium.edu/learning_studio/cow_eye/index.html

This site offers a complete lab on cow eye dissection.

States of Consciousness

Circadian Rhythms

http://www-nw.rz.uni-regensburg.de/~.tam14205.zoologie.biologie.uni-regensburg.de/CHRONO.HTM

This web site is dedicated to the study of circadian rhythms.

part

2

Sleep Disorders

http://www.sleepnet.com/disorder.htm

All of the common sleep disorders are discussed at this site.

Dreams

http://www.dreamgate.com/dream/resources/online97.htm

A massive site that contains Mail List, Usenet Newsgroups, and Web sites by Category: Dream Sharing, Magazines and Journals, Information, Education and Organizations, Personal Dream Journals, Religion, Spirituality and Healing (and Shamanism), Lucid Dreaming, Psi, Paranormal, Telepathic Dreaming, Dream Science and Research, Dreams and Anthropology, Dream Bibliography Collections, Dream Art, Dream Software, Jung and Dreams, Freud and Dreams, Books and Articles Online, and Lists of Links

World Sleep Home Pages

`http://bisleep.medsch.ucla.edu/`

The Sleep home pages provide a comprehensive resource for individuals who are involved in the research or treatment of sleep and sleep-related disorders.

Substance Use and Abuse

`http://orion.it.luc.edu/~pcrowe/375link.htm`

Links from a course at Loyola University taught on addiction/substance abuse are found at this site. It includes many diverse links from varying view points on this state of consciousness.

Memory and Learning

Behavior Analysis at the University of South Florida

`http://www.coedu.usf.edu/behavior/behavior.html`

The main purpose of this home page is to provide a low-response cost outlet to some of the interesting sources available on the Internet relating to behavioral analysis. Additionally, a listing of graduate training in behavioral analysis is provided.

History of Classical Conditioning

`http://www.as.wvu.edu/~sbb/comm221/chapters/`
`pavlov.htm`

This site has a detailed description of the history of classical conditioning.

Behavior Analysis Listservs

`http://www.coedu.usf.edu/behavior/listserv.html`

This is a listserv.

Common Cents

`http://www.exploratorium.edu/memory/index.html`

This site presents experiments in memory from the Exploratorium in San Francisco on memory for United States pennies.

Modern Classical Conditioning

`http://www.biozentrum.uni-wuerzburg.de/~brembs/classical/rwmodel.html`

The modern view by Rescorla and Wagner's of classical conditioning is presented at this site.

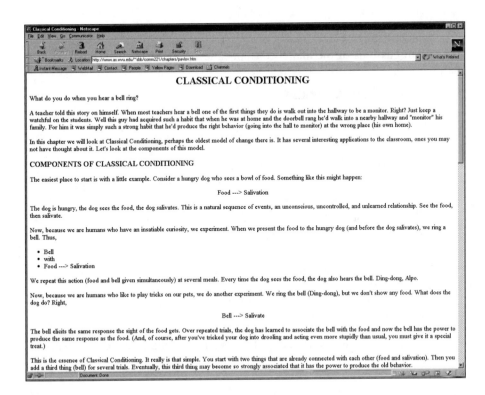

part

2

Cognitive Learning

```
http://bobcat.oursc.k12.ar.us/~jdharris/
cogmem.html
```

A text only discussion of cognitive learning can be found at this site.

Structures in Memory

```
http://www.mines.u-nancy.fr/~gueniffe/CoursEMN/I31/
ILS/e_for_e/nodes/NODE-8-pg.html
```

This site attempts to understand the variety of structures we have in our memories. There are many links to help define the discussion of structures of memory.

Behaviorism

```
http://129.7.160.115/inst5931/Behaviorism.html
```

Behaviorism as a learning theory is traced thought history. Also included are discussions of the major concepts and figures in Behaviorism.

Positive Reinforcement

```
http://server.bmod.athabascau.ca/html/prtut/
reinpair.htm
```

The purpose of this exercise is to teach the concept of positive reinforcement. In the first part of this exercise, the concept of positive reinforcement is defined and illustrated. In the second part of this exercise, you will classify fourteen examples and nonexamples and are given feedback about their performance.

Overview of Behavioral Psychology

```
http://www.valdosta.peachnet.edu/~whuitt/psy702/
behsys/behsys.html
```

This site discusses theories and defines terms in the behavioral perspective of learning.

part
2

Improving Memory Study Skills

```
http://www.gac.peachnet.edu/Student_life/
study_skills/effstdy.htm
```

There are a variety of study systems available, but all are organized in basically the same way and are designed to accomplish the same end: maximizing one's retention of information.

Classical Conditioning

```
http://www.indiana.edu/~iuepsyc/P103/lear/
lear.html
```

Examples and demonstrations of classical and operant conditioning are found at this site.

Cognition and Intelligence

The Center for Neural Basis of Cognition

```
http://www.cnbc.cmu.edu/
```

Many links to other sites on science of cognition may be found at this site.

Literature, Cognition, and the Brain

```
http://www2.bc.edu/~richarad/lcb/home.html
```

This web page features research at the intersection of literary studies, cognitive theory, and neuroscience.

Brain and Cognition Journal

```
http://www.apnet.com/www/journal/br.htm
```

A journal of clinical, experimental, and theoretical research, this site publishes original research articles, theoretical papers, critical reviews, case histories, historical articles, and scholarly notes.

IQ tests

http://www.2h.com/Tests/iqtrad.phtml

Large number of IQ tests, puzzles, and practice items all in the area of intelligence testing may be found at this site.

Alternative IQ

http://www.2h.com/Tests/iqalt.phtml

This site tests alternative IQ, with some humorous tests that include tests of your romance, jewelry, and garbage IQs.

Test of Intelligence

http://www.geocities.com/CapitolHill/1641/iqown.html

This site offers a traditional test of intelligence, with answers provided.

Cognitive Psychology

http://www.haverford.edu/psych/CogPsycpage.html

Cognitive Psychology Resources on the Web is sponsored by Haverford College, and includes many demonstrations and experiments.

Artificial Intelligence Subject Index

http://ai.iit.nrc.ca/misc.html

This extremely large site has links to all phases of artificial intelligence, including newsgroups, other sites bibliographies and data bases.

Cognitive Science Resources on the Internet

http://casper.beckman.uiuc.edu/~c-tsai4/cogsci/

Cognitive science is the study of intelligence and intelligent systems. This site has many links to help define this area of study.

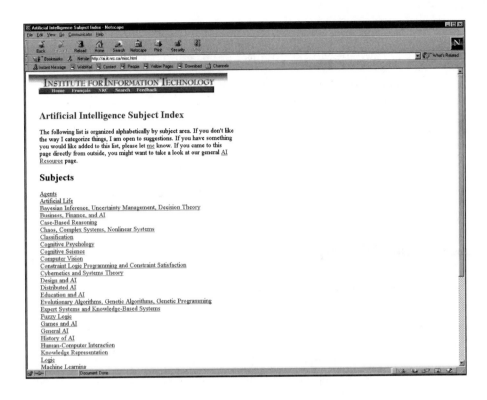

part

2

Braintainment Center

`http://www.brain.com/`

This is a large and interesting page that contains several activities centered around the theme of studying and enhancing intelligence. This site is famous for the five minute IQ test.

Creativity Web

`http://www.ozemail.com.au/~caveman/Creative/`

Resources for creativity and innovation may be found at this site.

IQ

`http://www.cycad.com/cgibin/Upstream/Issues/`
`psychology/IQ/index.html`

This site contains many links to controversial individuals and concepts in IQ, and may contain subject material that is controversial to some individuals.

The Intelligence Page

`http://www.netlink.co.uk/users/vess/mensal.html`

Many international links on intelligence, including many international Mensa links may be found at this site.

Cognitive Learning

`http://bobcat.oursc.k12.ar.us/~jdharris/cogmem.html`

This site offers a text-only discussion of cognitive learning.

Motivation and Emotion

The Diet and Weight Loss Page

`http://www1.mhv.net/~donn/diet.html`

This site offers many links related to diet, weight loss, and eating disorders. A tremendous amount of money and effort are spent each year to try to change our appearance. This page summarizes many topics associated with diet and weight loss.

Motivation

`http://choo.fis.utoronto.ca/FIS/Courses/LIS1230/`
`LIS1230sharma/motive4.htm`

A discussion of several theories of motivation may be found at this site.

Go Ask Alice

`http://www.goaskalice.columbia.edu/`

This site offers discussions of real life sexual motivations.

Anger

`http://www.apa.org/pubinfo/anger.html`

Anger is an emotional state that varies in intensity from mild irritation to intense fury and rage. Like other emotions, it is accompanied by physiological and biological changes. This site explores the varied aspects of the emotion anger.

Emotions and Emotional Intelligence

```
http://trochim.human.cornell.edu/gallery/young/
emotion.htm#emotions
```

This site is an on-line bibliography in the area of emotions and emotional intelligence, describing current research findings and notes of interest.

Motivation and Emotions

```
http://lucs.fil.lu.se/Staff/Christian.Balkenius/
Thesis/Chapter06.html
```

This site investigates the role of motivation as a determinant of behavior and learning. It discusses how motivation and emotion play an important role in cognitive processes in ways which have often been overlooked in the past.

part

2

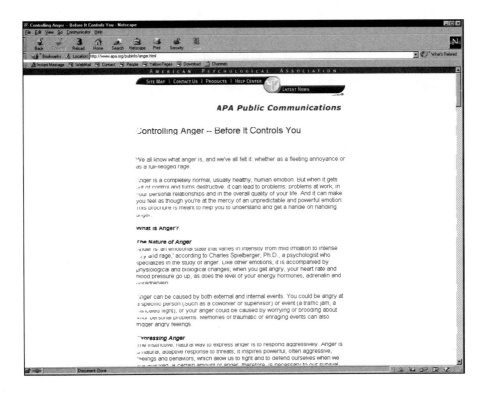

Abraham Maslow

http://sol.brunel.ac.uk/~jarvis/bola/motivation/
masmodel.html

Abraham Maslow Need-Satisfaction Model of Motivation is discussed at this site. Maslow is one of the major figures in the study on need-satisfaction in this century.

Child and Adolescent Development

Erikson's Theory of Development

http://idealist.com/children/erk.html

This site consists of a discussion of Erikson's stages of psychosocial development.

Kohlberg's Moral Stages

http://www.awa.com/w2/erotic_computing/kohlberg.
stages.html

This site discusses how Kolberg's theory specifies six stages of moral development, arranged in three levels.

Adolescent Development

http://www.yale.edu/ynhti/curriculum/units/1991/
5/91.05.07.x.html

This site discusses the physiological and psychological development of the adolescent.

Pregnancy and Early Care

http://www.parentsplace.com/genobject.cgi/readroom/
pregnant.html

This extensive site includes many discussions and links on the topics of pregnancy and early care for infants.

Young Children

http://www.earlychildhood.com/

The source of information for all who share an interest in improving the education and general life experience of young children, this is a place for getting advice from experts in the early childhood field, expanding your collection of creative projects, and sharing ideas and questions with the early childhood community.

Classic Theories of Child Development

http://idealist.com/children/

This large site includes tutorials on theory (a discussion of the classic theories of child development), and a key word search engine.

Adolescence Directory Online

http://education.indiana.edu/cas/adol/adol.html

Adolescence Directory On-Line (ADOL) is an electronic guide to information on adolescent issues. It is a service of the Center for Adolescent Studies at Indiana University for use by educators, counselors, parents, researchers, health, practitioners, and teens.

part

2

The Parent's Page

http://www.efn.org/~djz/birth/babylist.html

An extensive listing of traditional and nontraditional birthing, parenting, and pregnancy issues can be found at this site.

Midwifery, Pregnancy, Birth, and Breast-feeding

http://www.efn.org/~djz/birth/birthindex.html

Links and articles on midwifery, pregnancy, birth, and breast-feeding are available at this site.

Adolescence: Change and Continuity

http://www.personal.psu.edu/faculty/n/x/nxd10/adolesce.htm

This Website provides an introduction to some of the developmental changes that shape our lives between puberty and the end of college.

Although each life unfolds in its own unique pattern, this site provides information about the ways biological, psychological, and sociological influences systematically combine to shape its course.

Emotional Development

```
http://rock.uwc.edu/psych/psy360/outlines/
Socinf.htm
```

This site discusses the social and emotional development in infancy and toddlerhood

Piaget

```
http://www.piaget.org/biography/biog.html
```

This site is a short biography of Jean Piaget.

Vygotsky on Development

```
http://rock.uwc.edu/psych/psy360/outlines/
Cogearl.htm
```

Vygotsky's sociocultural view of development is covered at this site.

Language Development

```
http://www.parentingme.com/language.htm
```

This is a site dedicated to the understanding of language development.

Adult Development

National Institute on Aging (NIA)

```
http://www.nih.gov/nia/
```

The National Institute on Aging (NIA) is one of the National Institutes of Health, the principal biomedical research agency of the United States Government. The NIA promotes healthy aging by conducting and supporting biomedical, social, and behavioral research and public education.

Adult Development

http://www.css.edu/depts/grad/nia/index.htm

Research training in the psychology of aging can be found at this site.

The Society for Research in Adult Development

http://www.norwich.edu/srad/index.html

The international membership of the Society for Research in Adult Development includes individuals from all disciplines who are interested in positive adult development.

APA Division 20

http://www.iog.wayne.edu/apadiv20/study.htm

This site is an APA guide to graduate study in the psychology of adult development and aging.

part

2

Confusion in the Elderly

http://uhs.bsd.uchicago.edu/uhs/topics/delirium.dementia.html

This site defines and discusses Dementia, Delirium, and Depression in elderly populations.

Administration on Aging

http://www.aoa.dhhs.gov/

This Department of Health and Human Services site on the Administration on Aging offers extensive links to government services and other sites. It is a good site to explore the graying of America.

Family Relations

http://www.personal.psu.edu/faculty/n/x/nxd10/family3.htm

Although each family has its own unique pattern, this Website, containing extensive links developed by a class at Penn State University, will help users explore the ways that biological, psychological, and cultural influences systematically combine to shape family functioning.

American Psychological Association Division 20
Adult Development and Aging

http://www.iog.wayne.edu/APADIV20/lowdiv20.htm

These are the official World Wide Web Pages of the American Psychological Association's Division 20. This division is dedicated to studying the psychology of adult development and aging.

 # Personality

Major Personality Theorists

http://www.wynja.com/personality/theorists.html

This site includes many of the major personality theorists, with detailed material on their theories.

The Personality Project

http://fas.psych.nwu.edu/personality.html

These pages are meant to guide those interested in personality theory and research to the current personality research literature.

Personality

http://bill.psyc.anderson.edu/perth/freud.htm

Extensive links to major individuals and theories in the study of personality are available at this site.

Carl Rogers

http://psy1.clarion.edu/jms/Rogers.html

This site discusses Carl Rogers and his views on the therapeutic relationship.

Personality Test

http://www.2h.com/Tests/personality.phtml

This site contain a large selection of personality test that you can take on the Internet. Including test of anxiety, self esteem, attention deficient and type A personality.

Do You Have a Type A Personality?

http://www.queendom.com/typea2.html

An online personality test, containing seventeen items, which attempts to differentiate between A- and B-type personalities.

Foundations of Personality

http://www.haverford.edu/psych/ddavis/p109g/
p109g99.html

This hypertextual document provides a variety of Internet resources in an easily-accessible way. This site is a course in the department of psychology Haverford College but still contains useful information.

part

2

Jung Home Page

http://www.cgjung.com/cgjung/

In-depth analysis of Jung, and his theories, life, and contributions to psychology during this century with many articles and links.

Classical Adlerian Psychology

http://ourworld.compuserve.com/homepages/hstein/

Classical Adlerian psychology is a values-based, fully-integrated theory of personality, model of psychopathology, philosophy of living, strategy for preventative education, and techniques of psychotherapy.

FreudNet

`http://plaza.interport.net/nypsan/`

Linked sites dealing with the life's work of Freud, and his theories and contributions to psychology in the first half of this century.

The Keirsey Temperament Sorter

`http://www.keirsey.com/cgi-bin/keirsey/newkts.cgi`

The Keirsey Temperament Sorter by David Keirsey is a personality test which scores results according to the Myers-Briggs system (the actual Myers-Briggs test is a professional instrument and may only be administered by a licensed practitioner).

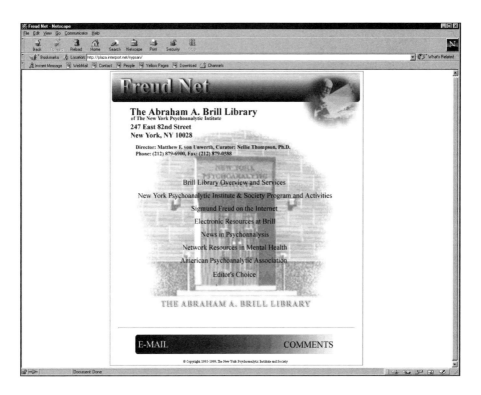

Stress and Health

Go Ask Alice

http://www.goaskalice.columbia.edu/

This site contains the Health Education and Wellness program of the Columbia University Health Service. This site is committed to helping individuals make choices that will contribute to their personal health and happiness, and to the well-being of others.

The Longevity Game

http://www.northwesternmutual.com/games/longevity/

This game determines how long one can expect to live based on one's current life style. This site is also listed as an activity.

Stress

http://www.w3.org/vl/Stress/

This WWW Virtual Library on Stress includes stress related links: a mix of commercial, government, and non-profit web sites and resources.

part

2

Stress and Health

http://psych.wisc.edu/faculty/pages/croberts/topic12.html

This site reviews several major systems of personality trait description within the context of exploring what personality is and how it relates to stress, health, and psychopathology.

Social Anxiety Test

http://www.queendom.com/soc_anx2.html

An online social anxiety test containing twenty-five items is offered at this site.

What is Stress?

`http://www.ivf.com/stress.html`

This site describes stress as the "wear and tear" our bodies experience as we adjust to our continually changing environment; it has physical and emotional effects on us and can create positive or negative feelings. Techniques for stress management and reductions are discussed.

Endocrinology and Stress-Related Disease

`http://www.endo-society.org/pubaffai/factshee/`
`stressrd.htm`

This site discusses how stress can cause or worsen some of our most common killers—cancer, heart disease, and cerebrovascular disease—and how it is directly related to other common disorders such as colitis, impotence, and depression.

The Society of Behavioral Medicine

`http://psychweb.syr.edu/sbm/sisterorg.html`

Extensive links to psychology sources, government sources, and public health sites, including public health, psychology, and medicine can be found at this site.

The Post Traumatic Stress Resources Web Page

`http://www.long-beach.va.gov/ptsd/stress.html`

The purpose of the Post Traumatic Stress Web Resources Page is to list and maintain information and links to professional information on Post Traumatic Stress Syndrome.

The National Clearinghouse for Alcohol and Drug Information

`http://www.health.org/`

This site offers links to prevention and treatment of substance abuse. PREVLINE offers electronic access to searchable databases and substance abuse prevention materials that pertain to alcohol, tobacco, and drugs

Psychological Disorders and Treatment

The Phobia List

http://www.sonic.net/~fredd/phobia1.html

This site includes a complete listing of phobias.

Psychological Assessment Categories

http://www.apa.org/books/mmpi.html

A series of articles on assessment are available at this site.

DSM-IV

http://uhs.bsd.uchicago.edu/~bhsiung/tips/dsm4n.html

A complete listing of the DSM-IV criteria can be found at this site.

part

2

Pharmacological Treatment of Social Phobia

http://uhs.bsd.uchicago.edu/dr-bob/tips/social.html#English

This site offers in-depth discussion of social phobias and their pharmacological treatment.

Schizoid Personality Disorder

http://mentalhelp.net/disorders/sx30.htm

This site describes the symptoms of Schizoid personality disorder.

National Anxiety Society

http://lexington-on-line.com/naf.html

This site contains many links of the topic of anxiety disorders.

Bi-Polar Disorder

http://bipolar.cmhc.com/

This is a site that includes the symptoms, treatments, and online support groups for Bi-polar disorder.

The Efficacy of Psychotherapy

http://www.apa.org/practice/peff.html

This site discusses the benefits of psychotherapy in 475 controlled studies, using only studies of patients seeking treatment for neuroses, true phobias, and emotional-somatic complaints. Statistical analysis of the data are discussed.

part

2

Behavior Therapy

http://site.health-center.com/brain/therapy/
default.htm

This site discusses how Behavior therapy focuses on what we do. This type of therapy works particularly well for problems in which certain maladaptive anxiety-causing behaviors recur such as phobias, anxiety disorders, obsessive-compulsive disorders, drug and alcohol problems, and eating disorders.

Interpersonal Therapy

http://site.health-
center.com/brain/therapy/default.htm

This site discusses Interpersonal therapy (IPT) which was developed for the treatment of depression. IPT has been empirically studied and has been shown, when used in conjunction with medication, to be superior to no active treatment and to medication alone.

part
2

Cognitive Therapy

http://site.health-center.com/brain/therapy/
default.htm

This site discusses how Cognitive psychotherapy focuses on identifying and changing negative thinking patterns. Often people with clinical depression make negative assumptions about their world. These assumptions lead them to have negative thoughts about themselves, their situation, and their future. These negative thoughts can create depressive feelings.

Internet Depression Resources List

http://www.blarg.net/~charlatn/Depression.html

This site includes links, discussion groups, helpgroups, and a comprehensive listing of site and resources on all types of mood disorders.

Eating Disorder

http://www.edap.org/

This homepage provides some basic information about Eating Disorders, awareness, prevention, and eating disorders in general.

The Anxiety Panic Internet Resource

`http://www.algy.com/anxiety/index.shtml`

This site is for people interested in anxiety disorders such as panic attacks, phobias, shyness, generalized anxiety, obsessive-compulsive behavior and post traumatic stress.

Doctor's Guide to Schizophrenia

`http://www.pslgroup.com/SCHIZOPHR. HTM`

This site offers the latest medical news and information for patients or friends/parents of patients diagnosed with schizophrenia and schizophrenia-related disorders.

Sleep Disorders

`http://www.sleepnet.com/disorder.htm`

This site contains everything you wanted to know about sleep disorders but were too tired to ask.

part

2

Obsessive-Compulsive Disorder

`http://www.iglou.com/fairlight/ocd/`

This site contains links to other sites, help groups and bulletin boards.

Mood disorders FAQ

`http://www.psych.helsinki.fi/~janne/asdfaq/`

This FAQ on mood disorders includes extensive links to on-line services, sites, and book lists. It is a must for anyone who has symptoms or knows family or friends with symptoms.

Schizophrenia

`http://www.mentalhealth.com/dis/p20-ps01.html`

General information and links on schizophrenia, is available at this site, including description, research, and treatment.

Psychiatry Information for the General Public

http://www.med.nyu.edu/Psych/public.html

This site offers on-line testing and screening for disorders from NYU Department of Psychiatry Home Page.

Depression Central

http://www.psycom.net/depression.central.html

This site is the Internet's central clearing house for information on all types of depressive disorders and on the most effective treatments for individuals suffering from major depression, manic-depression (bipolar disorder), cyclothymia, dysthymia, and other mood disorders.

Schizophrenia

http://www.mentalhealth.com/book/p40-sc02.html

This detailed site, produced by the British Columbia Friends of Schizophrenia Society, is one of the major reference sites on schizophrenia in the world.

part

2

BPD Central

http://www.bpdcentral.com/

Borderline Personality Disorder (BPD) is a major disorder in the personality disorders and anyone knowing someone so diagnosed should view this site, which offers listings of links for BPD.

Alzheimer's Disease

http://www.biostat.wustl.edu/alzheimer/

The Alzheimer's Page is an educational service created and sponsored by the Washington University Alzheimer's Disease Research Center.

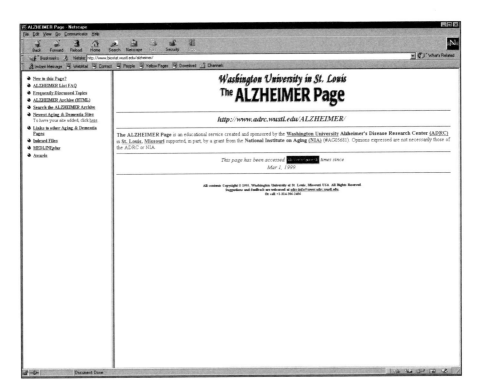

MentalHealth.Com

http://www.mentalhealth.com/p.html

Internet Mental Health, a free encyclopedia of mental health information. The goal of Internet Mental Health is to promote improved understanding, diagnosis, and treatment of mental illness throughout the world.

Emotional Support Groups on the Internet

http://www.lib.ox.ac.uk/internet/news/faq/archive/support.emotional.resources-list.html

This site is a list of resources for emotional support on the Internet and interconnected systems

DSM Criteria

http://www.apa.org/science/lib.html

This extensive APA site consists of terms and definitions of DSM criteria and describes all of what is currently considered to be abnormal behavior by the American Psychiatric Association.

Two Views on Diagnostic Books

http://www.apa.org/journals/nietzel.html

This is an APA site that discusses of the pros and cons of the DSM series.

Social Psychology

Power of Persuasion in Art

http://wae.clever.net/webcat/powers/powers.htm

This online exhibit features eleven posters and one sound file from a more extensive exhibit that was presented in the National Archives Building in Washington, DC on persuasion.

Research on Conformity

http://www.science.wayne.edu/~wpoff/cor/grp/
conformt.html

Definitions and research on conformity are presented at this site.

The Foot-in-the-Door

http://www.science.wayne.edu/~wpoff/cor/grp/
complian.html

Compliance and *The Foot-in-the-Door* tactic are detailed at this site.

Attraction and Love

http://www.telecom.csuhayward.edu/~psy3500/
key03a.html

Different stages of attraction and love are described at this site.

National Civil Rights Museum

http://mecca.org/~crights/cyber.html

Reducing prejudice and discrimination is the goal of this site.

Locus of Control Test

http://www.queendom.com/lc2.html

This test assesses your locus of control orientation and your attributional style with forty-two items. A locus of control orientation is a belief about whether the outcomes of our actions are contingent on what we do (internal control orientation) or on events outside our personal control (external control orientation).

part
2

Social Psychology Network

http://www.socialpsychology.org/

This page contains links to the major topics in social psychology. It is a very good starting place for any new student to the field of social psychology.

Compendium of Social Psychology Web Resources

http://cac.psu.edu/~arm3/social.html

Social psychology resources and social psychology programs and researchers are listed here.

Jumping Off Place for Social Psychologists.

http://swix.ch/clan/ks/CPSP1.htm#b_b

This site shows links to psychology-related resources available on the Internet. The links listed focus mostly on social psychology issues, but also consider other psychological topics such as clinical psychology.

Applied Psychology

Sports Psychology

http://www.demon.co.uk/mindtool/page11.html

This is a massive page with many links in the area of sports psychology.

Human Factors and the FAA

http://www.hf.faa.gov/

This site provides the aviation community and other interested users with information about human factors research and applications under the auspices of the National Plan for Civil Aviation Human Factors

I/O

http://www.siop.org/Instruct/InGuide.htm

This detailed guide to the sub fields of industrial/organizational psychology.

I/O Survival Guide

http://allserv.rug.ac.be/~flievens/guide.htm

This guide provides a plethora of internet sites valuable to the understanding of the field of industrial and organizational psychology.

Forensic Psychiatry

http://ua1vm.ua.edu/~jhooper/

Forensic psychiatry resource page contains links to other sites in the area.

part

2

Zeno's Forensic Page

`http://forensic.to/forensic.html`

This is a large site with many links in the area of forensic psychology.

CUErgo

`http://ergo.human.cornell.edu/`

Cornell's Human Factors and Ergonomics Program focuses on ways to improve comfort, performance, and health through the ergonomic design of products and environments.

Human Factors Home Page

`http://www.aviation.uiuc.edu/institute/acadProg/`
`epjp/humFacsites/hotlist.html`

This is a complete listing of interesting human factors sites maintained at University of Illinois at Urbana-Champaign.

part
2

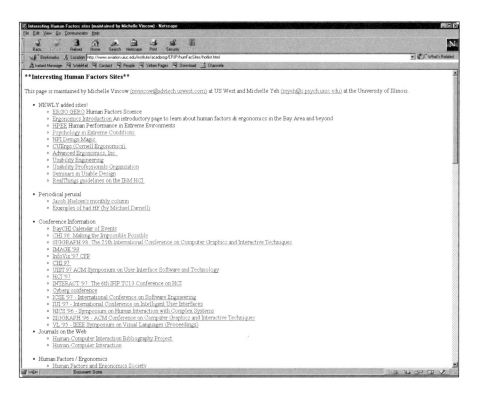

Sports and Exercise Psychology

http://spot.colorado.edu/~collinsj/

This site includes listings of organizations, graduate programs, and mailing lists for sports and exercise psychology. See related activity.

The Forensic Science Society

http://www.demon.co.uk/forensic/fortop.html

This is the home page for the Forensic Science Society. The Forensic Science Society is interested in the origins of forensic science and careers in forensic science in the UK.

The Journal of Environmental Psychology

http://www.apnet.com/www/journal/ps.htm

The Journal of Environmental Psychology is directed toward individuals in a wide range of disciplines who have an interest in the study of the transactions and interrelationships between people and their sociophysical surroundings (including man-made and natural environments) and the relation of this field to other social and biological sciences and to the environmental professions.

part

2

Environmental Psychology

http://www.snre.umich.edu/~rdeyoung/
envtpsych.html

This site offers an article on environmental psychology.

Human Factors at NASA

http://human-factors.arc.nasa.gov/

The NASA mission for this section is to develop a world-class center for human factors research, and to promote the broadest possible application of this research.

Documentation

 Your Citation for Exemplary Research

There's another detail left for us to handle—the formal citing of electronic sources in academic papers. The very factor that makes research on the Internet exciting is the same factor that makes referencing these sources challenging: their dynamic nature. A journal article exists, either in print or on microfilm, virtually forever. A document on the Internet can come, go, and change without warning. Because the purpose of citing sources is to allow another scholar to retrace your argument, a good citation allows a reader to obtain information from your primary sources, to the extent possible. This means you need to include not only information on when a source was posted on the Internet (if available) but also when you obtained the information.

The two arbiters of form for academic and scholarly writing are the Modern Language Association (MLA) and the American Psychological Association (APA); both organizations have established styles for citing electronic publications.

part
2

MLA Style

In the fifth edition of the *MLA Handbook for Writers of Research Papers,* the MLA recommends the following formats:

■ **URLs:** URLs are enclosed in angle brackets (<>) and contain the access mode identifier, the formal name for such indicators as "http" or "ftp." If a URL must be split across two lines, break it only after a slash (/). Never introduce a hyphen at the end of the first line. The URL should include all the parts necessary to identify uniquely the file/document being cited.

```
<http://www.csun.edu/~rtvfdept/home/index.html>
```

■ **An online scholarly project or reference database:** A complete online reference contains the title of the project or database (underlined); the name of the editor of the project or database (if given);

electronic publication information, including version number (if relevant and if not part of the title), date of electronic publication or latest update, and name of any sponsoring institution or organization; date of access; and electronic address.

The Perseus Project. Ed. Gregory R. Crane.
    Mar. 1997. Dept. of Classics, Tufts U.
    15 June 1998 <http://www.perseus.tufts.edu/>.

If you cannot find some of the information, then include the information that is available. The MLA also recommends that you print or download electronic documents, freezing them in time for future reference.

- **A document within a scholarly project or reference database:** It is much more common to use only a portion of a scholarly project or database. To cite an essay, poem, or other short work, begin this citation with the name of the author and the title of the work (in quotation marks). Then include all the information used when citing a complete online scholarly project or reference database, however, make sure you use the URL of the specific work and not the address of the general site.

part

2

Cuthberg, Lori. "Moonwalk: Earthlings' Finest Hour."
    Discovery Channel Online. 1999. Discovery
    Channel. 25 Nov. 1999 <http://www.discovery.com/
    indep/newsfeatures/moonwalk/challenge.html>.

- **A professional or personal site:** Include the name of the person creating the site (reversed), followed by a period, the title of the site (underlined), or, if there is no title, a description such as *Home page* (such a description is neither placed in quotes nor underlined). Specify the name of any school, organization, or other institution affiliated with the site and follow it with your date of access and the URL of the page.

Packer, Andy. Home page. 1 Apr. 1998
    <http://www.suu.edu/~students/Packer.htm>

Some electronic references are truly unique to the online domain. These include email, newsgroup postings, MUDs (multiuser domains) or MOOs (multiuser domains, object-oriented), and IRCs (Internet Relay Chats).

Email   In citing email messages, begin with the writer's name (reversed) followed by a period, and the title of the message (if any) in quotations as it appears in the subject line. Next comes a description of the message, typically "Email to," and the recipient (e.g., "the author"), and finally the date of the message.

```
Davis, Jeffrey. "Web Writing Resources." Email to
    Nora Davis. 3 Jan. 2000.

Sommers, Laurice. "Re: College Admissions Practices."
    Email to the author. 12 Aug. 1998.
```

List Servers and Newsgroups   In citing these references, begin with the author's name (reversed) followed by a period. Next include the title of the document (in quotes) from the subject line, followed by the words "Online posting" (not in quotes). Follow this with the date of posting. For list servers, include the date of access, the name of the list (if known), and the online address of the list's moderator or administrator. For newsgroups, follow "Online posting" with the date of posting, the date of access, and the name of the newsgroup, prefixed with "news:" and enclosed in angle brackets.

```
Applebaum, Dale. "Educational Variables." Online
    posting. 29 Jan. 1998. Higher Education
    Discussion Group. 30 Jan. 1993
    <jlucidoj@unc.edu>.

Gostl, Jack. "Re: Mr. Levitan." Online posting.
    13 June 1997. 20 June 1997
    <news:alt.edu.bronxscience>.
```

MUDs, MOOs, and IRCs   Begin with the name of the speaker(s) followed by a period. Follow with the description and date of the event, the forum in which the communication took place, the date of access, and the online address prefixed by "telnet://".

```
Guest. Personal interview. 13 Aug. 1998.
    <telnet://du.edu:8888>.
```

For more information on MLA documentation style, check out their Web site at http://www.mla.org/set_stl.htm

APA Style

The *Publication Manual of the American Psychological Association* (4th ed.) is fairly dated in its handling of online sources, having been published before the rise of the WWW and the generally recognized format for URLs. The format that follows is based on the APA manual, with modifications. It's important to remember that, unlike the MLA, the APA does not include temporary or transient sources (e.g., letters, phone calls, etc.) in its "References" page, preferring to handle them in in-text citations exclusively. This rule holds for electronic sources as well: email, MOOs/MUDs, list server postings, etc., are not included in the "References" page, merely cited in text, for example, "But Wilson has rescinded his earlier support for these policies" (Charles Wilson, personal email to the author, 20 November 1996). But also note that many list server and Usenet groups and MOOs actually archive their correspondences, so that there is a permanent site (usually a Gopher or FTP server) where those documents reside. In that case, you would want to find the archive and cite it as an unchanging source. Strictly speaking, according to the APA manual, a file from an FTP site should be referenced as follows:

```
Deutsch, P. (1991). Archie: An electronic directory
    service for the Internet [Online]. Available FTP:
    ftp.sura.net Directory: pub/archie/docs File:
    whatis.archie.
```

However, the increasing familiarity of Net users with the convention of a URL makes the prose description of how to find a file ("Available FTP: ftp.sura.net Directory: pub/archie/docs File: whatis.archie") unnecessary.

So, modification of the APA format, (as suggested by the APA at its Web site—www.apa.org), citations from the standard Internet sources would appear as follows.

FTP (File Transfer Protocol) Sites To cite files available for downloading via FTP, give the author's name (if known), the publication date (if available and if different from the date accessed), the full title of the paper (capitalizing only the first word and proper nouns), the date of

part **2**

access, and the address of the FTP site along with the full path necessary to access the file.

```
Deutsch, P. (1991) Archie: An electronic directory
    service for the Internet. Retrieved January 25,
    2000 from File Transfer Protocol: ftp://
    ftp.sura.net/pub/archie/docs/whatis.archie
```

WWW Sites (World Wide Web) To cite files available for viewing or downloading via the World Wide Web, give the author's name (if known), the year of publication (if known and if different from the date accessed), the full title of the article, and the title of the complete work (if applicable) in italics. Include any additional information (such as versions, editions, or revisions) in parentheses immediately following the title. Include the date of retrieval and the full URL (the http address).

```
Burka, L. P. (1993). A hypertext history of multi-
    user dungeons. MUDdex. Retrieved January 13, 1997
    from the World Wide Web: http://www.utopia.com/
    talent/lpb/muddex/essay/

Tilton, J. (1995). Composing good HTML (Vers. 2.0.6).
    Retrieved December 1, 1996 from the World Wide Web:
    http://www.cs.cmu.edu/~tilt/cgh/
```

Synchronous Communications (MOOs, MUDs, IRC, etc.) Give the name of the speaker(s), the complete date of the conversation being referenced in parentheses, and the title of the session (if applicable). Next, list the title of the site in italics, the protocol and address (if applicable), and any directions necessary to access the work. Last, list the date of access, followed by the retrieval information. Personal interviews do not need to be listed in the References, but do need to be included in parenthetic references in the text (see the APA *Publication Manual*).

```
Cross, J. (1996, February 27). Netoric's Tuesday
    cafe: Why use MUDs in the writing classroom?
    MediaMoo. Retrieved March 1, 1996 from File
    Transfer Protocol: ftp://daedalus.com/
    pub/ACW/NETORIC/catalog
```

Gopher Sites List the author's name (if applicable), the year of publication, the title of the file or paper, and the title of the complete work (if applicable). Include any print publication information (if available) followed by the protocol (i.e., gopher://). List the date that the file was accessed and the path necessary to access the file.

```
Massachusetts Higher Education Coordinating
    Council. (1994). Using coordination
    and collaboration to address change. Retrieved
    July 16, 1999 from the World Wide Web:
    gopher://gopher.mass.edu:170/00gopher_root%3A%5B_
    hecc%5D_plan
```

Email, Listservs, and Newsgroups Do not include personal email in the list of References. Although unretrievable communication such as email is not included in APA References, somewhat more public or accessible Internet postings from newsgroups or listservs may be included. See the APA *Publication Manual* for information on in-text citations.

```
Heilke, J. (1996, May 3). Webfolios. Alliance for
    Computers and Writing Discussion List. Retrieved
    December 31, 1996 from the World Wide Web:
    http://www.ttu.edu/lists/acw-l/9605/0040.html
```

part

2

Other authors and educators have proposed similar extensions to the APA style, too. You can find URLs to these pages at

```
www.psychwww.com/resource/apacrib.htm
```

Another frequently-referenced set of extensions is available at

```
www.uvm.edu/~ncrane/estyles/apa.htm
```

Remember, "frequently-referenced" does not equate to "correct" or even "desirable." Check with your professor to see if your course or school has a preference for an extended APA style.

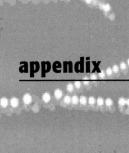

appendix

Listing of All URLs

Overview

Psychology Departments on the Web
http://www.psychwww.com/resource/deptlist.htm

Careers in psychology
http://www.psychwww.com/careers/index.htm

Experimental and Correlational Research
http://www.indiana.edu/~gasser/experiments.html

Ethics in Research
http://methods.fullerton.edu/chapter3.html

Gallup Polls
http://www.gallup.com/

Educational Testing Service
http://www.ets.org/

Code of Conduct
http://www.apa.org/ethics/code.html

Statistics on the Web
http://www.spss.com/StatsWeb/

The Lifschitz Psychology Museum
http://www.netaxs.com/people/aca3/LPM. HTM

The Mind Body Problem
http://serendip.brynmawr.edu/Mind/Table.html

Statistic Glossary
http://www.cas.lancs.ac.uk/glossary_v1.1/main.html

William James
http://serendip.brynmawr.edu/Mind/James.html

Psychological Research on the Net
http://psych.hanover.edu/APS/exponnet.html

Major Areas of Psychology
http://www.gasou.edu/psychweb/tipsheet/specialt.htm

Experimental Psychology
http://www.york.ac.uk/depts/psych/www/etc/whatispsych.html

Careers in Psychology
http://www.rider.edu/users/suler/gradschl.html

appendix

Today in the History of Psychology
http://www.cwu.edu/~warren/today.html

Usenet Newsgroups
http://www-psych.stanford.edu/cogsci/usenet.html

Biological Basis of Behavior

Basic Neural Processes Tutorials
http://psych.hanover.edu/Krantz/neurotut.html

Neuroscience on the Internet
http://www.neuroguide.com/index4.html#live

Neuropsychology Central
http://www.neuropsychologycentral.com/

Neurotransmission
http://www.csuchico.edu/psy/BioPsych/neurotransmission.html

Brain Imaging
http://www.bic.mni.mcgill.ca/demos/

Neuroscience
http://faculty.washington.edu/chudler/ehceduc.html

Genetics
http://www.med.jhu.edu/Greenberg.Center/tutorial.htm#basics

The Whole Brain Atlas
http://www.med.harvard.edu/AANLIB/home.html

The Visible Human Project
http://www.nlm.nih.gov/research/visible/visible_human.html

Human Brain Project
http://www-hbp.scripps.edu/

Human Genome Project
http://www.ornl.gov/TechResources/Human_Genome/home.html

Neuroscience
http://neuro.med.cornell.edu/VL/

Cognitive-Neuroscience Resources
http://www-cgi.cs.cmu.edu/afs/cs/project/cnbc/other/
other-neuro.html

McConnell Brain Imaging Center
http://www.bic.mni.mcgill.ca/

Split Brain
http://ezinfo.ucs.indiana.edu/~pietsch/split-brain.html

appendix

Sensation and Perception

Kinesthetic Child
http://www.latitudes.org/learn01.html

Subliminal Persuasion
http://www.yahoo.com/Science/Cognitive_Science/
Unconscious_Cognition/Subliminal_Perception/

Auditory Perception
http://neuro.bio.tu-darmstadt.de/langner/langner_e.html

Exploratorium
http://www.exploratorium.edu/imagery/exhibits.html

Historical Origins of Color Vision Research
http://kiptron.psyc.virginia.edu/steve_boker/ColorVision2/
node3.html

Illusionworks.
http://www.illusionworks.com/

Perception of Facial Aging Laboratory.
http://psych.st-and.ac.uk:8080/research/perception_lab/

**Kubovy Perception Lab University of Virginia
Department of Psychology**
http://minerva.acc.virginia.edu/~mklab/

University of California at Santa Cruz Perceptual Science Laboratory
http://mambo.ucsc.edu/

appendix

Vision Research WWW Servers
http://www.socsci.uci.edu/cogsci/vision.html

Auditory Perception
http://www.music.mcgill.ca/auditory/Auditory.html

The Joy of Visual Perception: A Web Book
http://www.yorku.ca/research/vision/eye/

International Symposium on Olfaction and Taste
http://www.psychology.sdsu.edu/ISOT/

Cow Eye Dissection
http://www.exploratorium.edu/learning_studio/cow_eye/
index.html

States of Consciousness

Circadian Rhythms
http://www-nw.rz.uni-regensburg.de/~.tam14205.zoologie.
biologie.uni-regensburg.de/CHRONO. HTM

Sleep Disorders
http://www.sleepnet.com/disorder.htm

Dreams
> http://www.dreamgate.com/dream/resources/online97.htm

World Sleep Home Pages
> http://bisleep.medsch.ucla.edu/

Substance Use and Abuse
> http://orion.it.luc.edu/~pcrowe/375link.htm

Memory and Learning

Behavior Analysis at the University of South Florida
> http://www.coedu.usf.edu/behavior/behavior.html

History of Classical Conditioning
> http://www.as.wvu.edu/~sbb/comm221/chapters/pavlov.htm

Behavior Analysis List Servers
> http://www.coedu.usf.edu/behavior/listserv.html

Common Cents
> http://www.exploratorium.edu/memory/index.html

Modern Classical Conditioning
> http://www.biozentrum.uni-wuerzburg.de/~brembs/classical/
> rwmodel.html

Cognitive Learning
> http://bobcat.oursc.k12.ar.us/~jdharris/cogmem.html

Structures in Memory
> http://www.mines.u-nancy.fr/~gueniffe/CoursEMN/I31/
> ILS/e_for_e/nodes/NODE-8-pg.html

Behaviorism
> http://129.7.160.115/inst5931/Behaviorism.html

Positive Reinforcement
> http://server.bmod.athabascau.ca/html/prtut/reinpair.htm

Overview of Behavioral Psychology
> http://www.valdosta.peachnet.edu/~whuitt/psy702/behsys/
> behsys.html

Improving Memory Study Skills
http://www.gac.peachnet.edu/Student_life/study_skills/
effstdy.htm

Classical Conditioning
http://www.indiana.edu/~iuepsyc/P103/lear/lear.html

Cognition and Intelligence

The Center for Neural Basis of Cognition
http://www.cnbc.cmu.edu/

Literature, Cognition and the Brain
http://www2.bc.edu/~richarad/lcb/home.html

Brain and Cognition Journal
http://www.apnet.com/www/journal/br.htm

appendix

IQ tests
http://www.2h.com/Tests/iqtrad.phtml

Alternative IQ
http://www.2h.com/Tests/iqalt.phtml

Test of Intelligence
http://www.geocities.com/CapitolHill/1641/iqown.html

Cognitive Psychology
http://www.haverford.edu/psych/CogPsycpage.html

Artificial Intelligence Subject Index
http://ai.iit.nrc.ca/misc.html

Cognitive Science Resources on the Internet
http://casper.beckman.uiuc.edu/~c-tsai4/cogsci/

Braintainment Center
http://www.brain.com/

Creativity Web
http://www.ozemail.com.au/~caveman/Creative/

IQ
http://www.cycad.com/cgi-bin/Upstream/Issues/psychology/
IQ/index.html

The Intelligence Page
http://www.netlink.co.uk/users/vess/mensal.html

Cognitive Learning
http://bobcat.oursc.k12.ar.us/~jdharris/cogmem.html

Motivation and Emotion

The Diet and Weight Loss Page
http://www1.mhv.net/~donn/diet.html

Motivation
http://choo.fis.utoronto.ca/FIS/Courses/LIS1230/
LIS1230sharma/motive4.htm

Go Ask Alice
http://www.goaskalice.columbia.edu/

Anger
http://www.apa.org/pubinfo/anger.html

Emotions and Emotional Intelligence
http://trochim.human.cornell.edu/gallery/young/
emotion.htm#emotions

Motivation and Emotions
http://lucs.fil.lu.se/Staff/Christian.Balkenius/Thesis/
Chapter06.html

Abraham Maslow
http://sol.brunel.ac.uk/~jarvis/bola/motivation/masmodel.html

appendix

Child and Adolescent Development

Erikson's Theory of Development
http://idealist.com/children/erk.html

Kohlberg's Moral Stages
http://www.awa.com/w2/erotic_computing/kohlberg.stages.html

Adolescent Development
http://www.yale.edu/ynhti/curriculum/units/1991/5/
91.05.07.x.html

Pregnancy and Early Care
http://www.parentsplace.com/genobject.cgi/readroom/
pregnant.html

Young Children
http://www.earlychildhood.com/

Classic Theories of Child Development
http://idealist.com/children/

Adolescence Directory On-Line
http://education.indiana.edu/cas/adol/adol.html

The Parent's Page
http://www.efn.org/~djz/birth/babylist.html

Midwifery, Pregnancy, Birth, and Breast-feeding
http://www.efn.org/~djz/birth/birthindex.html

Adolescence: Change and Continuity
http://www.personal.psu.edu/faculty/n/x/nxd10/adolesce.htm

Emotional Development
http://rock.uwc.edu/psych/psy360/outlines/Socinf.htm

Piaget
http://www.piaget.org/biography/biog.html

Vygotsky on Development
http://rock.uwc.edu/psych/psy360/outlines/Cogearl.htm

Language Development
http://www.parentingme.com/language.htm

Adult Development

National Institute on Aging (NIA)
http://www.nih.gov/nia/

Adult Development
http://www.css.edu/depts/grad/nia/index.htm

The Society for Research in Adult Development
http://www.norwich.edu/srad/index.html

APA Division 20
http://www.iog.wayne.edu/apadiv20/study.htm

Confusion in the Elderly
http://uhs.bsd.uchicago.edu/uhs/topics/delirium.
dementia.html

Administration on Aging
http://www.aoa.dhhs.gov/

Family Relations
http://www.personal.psu.edu/faculty/n/x/nxd10/family3.htm

American Psychological Association Division 20 Adult
Development and Aging
http://www.iog.wayne.edu/APADIV20/lowdiv20.htm

Personality

Major Personality Theorists
http://www.wynja.com/personality/theorists.html

The Personality Project
http://fas.psych.nwu.edu/personality.html

Personality
http://bill.psyc.anderson.edu/perth/freud.htm

Carl Rogers
http://psy1.clarion.edu/jms/Rogers.html

Personality Test
http://www.2h.com/Tests/personality.phtml

Do You Have a Type A Personality?
http://www.queendom.com/typea2.html

Foundations of Personality
http://www.haverford.edu/psych/ddavis/p109g/
p109g99.html

Jung Home Page
  http://www.cgjung.com/cgjung/

Classical Adlerian Psychology
  http://ourworld.compuserve.com/homepages/hstein/

FreudNet
  http://plaza.interport.net/nypsan/

The Keirsey Temperament Sorter
  http://www.keirsey.com/cgi-bin/keirsey/newkts.cgi

Stress and Health

appendix

Go Ask Alice
  http://www.goaskalice.columbia.edu/

The Longevity Game
  http://www.northwesternmutual.com/games/longevity/

Stress
  http://www.w3.org/vl/Stress/

Stress and Health
  http://psych.wisc.edu/faculty/pages/croberts/topic12.html

Social Anxiety Test
  http://www.queendom.com/soc_anx2.html

What is Stress?
  http://www.ivf.com/stress.html

Endocrinology and Stress-Related Disease
  http://www.endo-society.org/pubaffai/factshee/stressrd.htm

The Society of Behavioral Medicine
  http://psychweb.syr.edu/sbm/sisterorg.html

The Post Traumatic Stress Resources Web Page
  http://www.long-beach.va.gov/ptsd/stress.html

The National Clearinghouse for Alcohol and Drug Information
http://www.health.org/

Psychological Disorders and Treatment

The Phobia List
http://www.sonic.net/~fredd/phobia1.html

Psychological Assessment Categories
http://www.apa.org/books/mmpi.html

DSM-IV
http://uhs.bsd.uchicago.edu/~bhsiung/tips/dsm4n.html

Pharmacological Treatment of Social Phobia
http://uhs.bsd.uchicago.edu/dr-bob/tips/
social.html#English

Schizoid Personality Disorder
http://mentalhelp.net/disorders/sx30.htm

National Anxiety Society
http://lexington-on-line.com/naf.html

Bi-Polar Disorder
http://bipolar.cmhc.com/

The Efficacy of Psychotherapy
http://www.apa.org/practice/peff.html

Behavior Therapy
http://site.health-center.com/brain/therapy/default.htm

Interpersonal Therapy
http://site.health-center.com/brain/therapy/default.htm

Cognitive Therapy
http://site.health-center.com/brain/therapy/default.htm

Internet Depression Resources List
http://www.blarg.net/~charlatn/Depression.html

Eating Disorder
http://www.edap.org/

The Anxiety Panic Internet Resource
http://www.algy.com/anxiety/index.shtml

Doctor's Guide to Schizophrenia
http://www.pslgroup.com/SCHIZOPHR. HTM

Sleep Disorders
http://www.sleepnet.com/disorder.htm

Obsessive-Compulsive Disorder
http://www.iglou.com/fairlight/ocd/

Mood Disorders FAQ
http://www.psych.helsinki.fi/~janne/asdfaq/

Schizophrenia
http://www.mentalhealth.com/dis/p20-ps01.html

appendix

Psychiatry Information for the General Public
http://www.med.nyu.edu/Psych/public.html

Depression Central
http://www.psycom.net/depression.central.html

Schizophrenia
http://www.mentalhealth.com/book/p40-sc02.html

BPD Central
http://www.bpdcentral.com/

Alzheimer's Disease
http://www.biostat.wustl.edu/alzheimer/

MentalHealth.Com
http://www.mentalhealth.com/p.html

Emotional Support Groups on the Internet
http://www.lib.ox.ac.uk/internet/news/faq/archive/
support.emotional.resources-list.html

DSM Criteria
http://www.apa.org/science/lib.html

Two Views on Diagnostic Books
http://www.apa.org/journals/nietzel.html

Social Psychology

Power of Persuasion in Art
http://wae.clever.net/webcat/powers/powers.htm

Research on Conformity
http://www.science.wayne.edu/~wpoff/cor/grp/conformt.html

The Foot-in-the-Door
http://www.science.wayne.edu/~wpoff/cor/grp/complian.html

Attraction and Love
http://www.telecom.csuhayward.edu/~psy3500/key03a.html

National Civil Rights Museum
http://mecca.org/~crights/cyber.html

Locus of Control Test
http://www.queendom.com/lc2.html

Social Psychology Network
http://www.socialpsychology.org/

Compendium of Social Psychology Web Resources
http://cac.psu.edu/~arm3/social.html

Jumping Off Place for Social Psychologists.
http://swix.ch/clan/ks/CPSP1.htm#b_b

Applied Psychology

Sports Psychology
http://www.demon.co.uk/mindtool/page11.html

Human Factors and the FAA
http://www.hf.faa.gov/

I/O
http://www.siop.org/Instruct/InGuide.htm

I/O Survival Guide
http://allserv.rug.ac.be/~flievens/guide.htm

Forensic Psychiatry
http://ua1vm.ua.edu/~jhooper/

Zeno's Forensic Page
http://forensic.to/forensic.html

CUErgo
http://ergo.human.cornell.edu/

Human Factors Home Page
http://www.aviation.uiuc.edu/institute/acadProg/epjp/
humFacsites/hotlist.html

Sports and Exercise Psychology
http://spot.colorado.edu/~collinsj/

The Forensic Science Society
http://www.demon.co.uk/forensic/fortop.html

The Journal of Environmental Psychology
http://www.apnet.com/www/journal/ps.htm

appendix

Environmental Psychology
http://www.snre.umich.edu/~rdeyoung/envtpsych.html

Human Factors at NASA
http://human-factors.arc.nasa.gov/

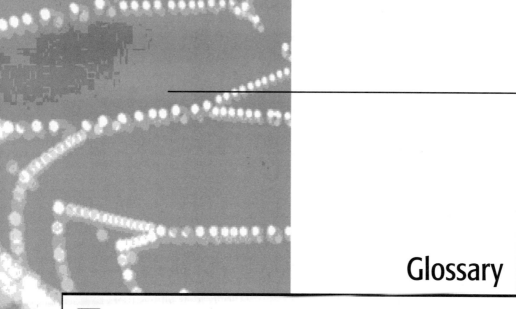

Glossary

Your Own Private Glossary

The Glossary in this book contains reference terms you'll find useful as you get started on the Internet. After a while, however, you'll find yourself running across abbreviations, acronyms, and buzzwords whose definitions will make more sense to you once you're no longer a novice (or "newbie"). That's the time to build a glossary of your own. For now, the 2DNet Webopædia gives you a place to start.

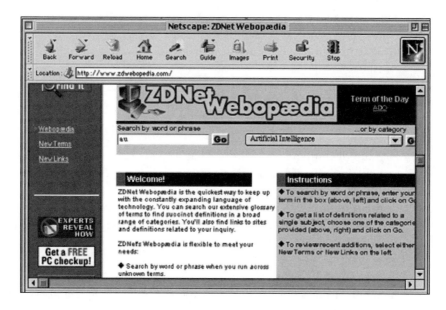

alias
A simple email address that can be used in place of a more complex one.

AVI
Audio Video Interleave. A video compression standard developed for use with Microsoft Windows. Video clips on the World Wide Web are usually available in both AVI and QuickTime formats.

bandwidth
Internet parlance for capacity to carry or transfer information such as email and Web pages.

BBS
Bulletin Board System. A dial-up computer service that allows users to post messages and download files. Some BBSs are connected to and provide access to the Internet, but many are self-contained.

browser
The computer program that lets you view the contents of Web sites.

client
A program that runs on your personal computer and supplies you with Internet services, such as getting your mail.

cyberspace
The whole universe of information that is available from computer networks. The term was coined by science fiction writer William Gibson in his novel *Neuromancer,* published in 1984.

DNS
See **domain name server.**

domain
A group of computers administered as a single unit, typically belonging to a single organization such as a university or corporation.

domain name
A name that identifies one or more computers belonging to a single domain. For example, "apple.com".

domain name server
A computer that converts domain names into the numeric addresses used on the Internet.

download
Copying a file from another computer to your computer over the Internet.

email
Electronic mail.

emoticon
A guide to the writer's feelings, represented by typed characters, such as the Smiley :-). Helps readers understand the emotions underlying a written message.

FAQ
Frequently Asked Questions

flame
A rude or derogatory message directed as a personal attack against an individual or group.

flame war
An exchange of flames (see above).

FTP
File Transfer Protocol, a method of moving files from one computer to another over the Internet.

home page
A page on the World Wide Web that acts as a starting point for information about a person or organization.

hypertext
Text that contains embedded *links* to other pages of text. Hypertext enables the reader to navigate between pages of related information by following links in the text.

LAN:
Local Area Network. A computer network that is located in a concentrated area, such as offices within a building.

link
A reference to a location on the Web that is embedded in the text of the Web page. Links are usually highlighted with a different color or underline to make them easily visible.

list server
Strictly speaking, a computer program that administers electronic mailing lists, but also used to denote such lists or discussion groups, as in "the writer's list server."

lurker
A passive reader of an Internet *newsgroup*. A lurker reads messages, but does not participate in the discussion by posting or responding to messages.

mailing list
A subject-specific automated e-mail system. Users subscribe and receive e-mail from other users about the subject of the list.

modem
A device for connecting two computers over a telephone line.

newbie
A new user of the Internet.

newsgroup
A discussion forum in which all participants can read all messages and public replies between the participants.

pages
All the text, graphics, pictures, and so forth, denoted by a single URL beginning with the identifier "http://".

plug-in
A third-party software program that will lend a web browser (Netscape, Internet Explorer, etc.) additional features.

quoted
Text in an email message or newsgroup posting that has been set off by the use of vertical bars or > characters in the left-hand margin.

search engine
A computer program that will locate Web sites or files based on specified criteria.

secure
A Web page whose contents are encrypted when sending or receiving information.

server
A computer program that moves information on request, such as a Web server that sends pages to your browser.

Smiley
See **emoticon.**

snail mail
Mail sent the old fashioned way: Write a letter, put it in an envelope, stick on a stamp, and drop it in the mailbox.

spam
Spam is to the Internet as unsolicited junk mail is to the postal system.

URL
Uniform Resource Locator: The notation for specifying addresses on the World Wide Web (e.g. http://www.abacon.com or ftp://ftp.abacon.com).

Usenet
The section of the Internet devoted to *newsgroups.*

Web browser
A program used to navigate and access information on the World Wide Web. Web browsers convert html coding into a display of pictures, sound, and words.

Web site
A collection of World Wide Web pages, usually consisting of a home page and several other linked pages.